EASTER
EARTHQUAKE

JAMES A. HARNISH

EASTER
EARTHQUAKE

HOW RESURRECTION
SHAKES OUR WORLD

UPPER
ROOM BOOKS®
NASHVILLE

Cover design: LUCAS Art & Design
Cover photo: Masterfile Images

ISBN: 978-0-8358-1716-5 (print); 978-0-8358-1717-2 (mobi);
     978-0-8358-1718-9 (epub)

For

JULIA, ALEX, LUKE, MATTIE, AND MOLLY

One generation will praise
God's works to the next one.

—Psalm 145:4

CONTENTS

There Was a Great Earthquake   9

The Invitation   15

Ash Wednesday: Beginning Where Our Stories End   19

First Week in Lent: Shaking the Powers   23

Second Week in Lent: Surprising Hope   37

Third Week in Lent: Beyond Belief   51

Fourth Week in Lent: Healing Scars   65

Fifth Week in Lent: New Life in the Graveyard   79

Holy Week: Descending into Glory   93

Easter: After the Earthquake   107

A Guide for Daily Meditation and Prayer   115

A Guide for Small-Group Gatherings   119

Notes   122

About the Author   125

There Was a Great Earthquake

The earth which trembled with horror at the death of
Christ, as it were leaped with joy at the resurrection.
> —Cornelius à Lapide (1567–1637)

Like a network reporter announcing "breaking" news,
Matthew reports that on the first Easter morning an
earthquake rocked the earth, ripped open the tomb, and scared
the living daylights out of the Roman guards who "shook with
fear and became like dead men" (Matt. 28:4, CEB).

This is the second earthquake recorded in Matthew's Gospel.
On the previous Friday, the noonday sky turned black. When
Jesus cried out, "My God, my God, why have you forsaken me?"
(Matt. 27:46) and took his last breath, "the earth shook, and the
rocks were split" (Matt. 27:51).

I've never experienced an earthquake, but a friend who was
in San Francisco when the quake hit in 1989 noted, "We take
for granted that the ground we walk on will always be there; but
during an earthquake, even the most basic of assumptions can't
be counted on."

Earthquakes shake our basic assumption that the *terra firma*
will stay firm, that the earth will remain steady beneath our

feet, that the world's current existence is the way it will always be. When the tectonic plates shift beneath the earth's surface and the ground shakes beneath our feet, it rattles the bedrock assumptions upon which we build our lives.

Whether the earthquakes show up on the Richter scale or not, some shake all of us: unexpected shifts in our relationships, unanticipated events that rock the norms by which we live. Sometimes the events are global: the day the World Trade Towers fell or the markets crashed. Sometimes they are deeply personal: the broken marriage vow, the cancer diagnosis, the ended career, the death of a loved one. When the earth shakes, we cry out, "My God, why have you forsaken me?"

That's where Matthew leaves the women on Friday night. They feel the earth shake as they watch Jesus die. They see Joseph place his battered, bloody body in the tomb carved into solid rock. They hear the stone roll across the entrance with a heavy, funereal thud. Pilate's guards place the seal of Rome on it and settle in to make sure that the body stays where it belongs. It is the end of Jesus' story. Everyone can return to the world and to their lives the way they had always been.

But then, the unexpected happens! As the new day dawns, a great earthquake occurs. An angel descends—the biblical sign of God's direct intrusion into human history—rolls back the stone, sits down, crosses his legs, dusts off his hands, and with a confident wink asks, "You got any larger stones around here?"

The earth itself leaps for joy with the good news that God has not forsaken Jesus. God shatters the all-too-predictable power of death with the unexpected power of new life. The same God who breathed life into dusty chaos on the first morning of creation breathes new life into the lifeless Jesus and brings forth a whole new creation.

The Easter earthquake invites us into a new creation: a creation not ruled by what Paul calls "the principalities and powers" of this world but by a creation that serves as the living expression of God's reign revealed in Jesus Christ that is becoming a reality on earth. In this new creation, the tomb does not signal the end of Jesus' story but the beginning of the reign of his love, grace, justice, and peace. Paul declares the good news, "If anyone is in Christ, there is a new creation: everything old has passed away; see, everything has become new!" (2 Cor. 5:17).

The Easter earthquake reverses the deadly, God-forsaken assumptions upon which far too much of our world and far too many of our lives operate. It invites us into a God-soaked world energized by the life-giving presence of the risen Christ.

The Easter earthquake
shakes our assumptions about our own lives.

There's a wonderfully personal element in the way Jesus meets the women and says, "Greetings!" One translation says, "Good morning." It reminds me of the way Australians say, "G'day!" or the British say, "Cheers!"

The earthshaking promise of Easter is that God has not forsaken any of us. The risen Christ will meet us along the confused, chaotic, fearful paths of our lives and speak the same words the women hear at the tomb, "Do not be afraid."

Too often we build our lives on the bedrock of fear: fear of terrorism, fear for the economy, fear of people who are different from us, fear of anything politicians tell us to fear in order to maintain power, fear of rejection, fear of sickness, fear of death. But the Resurrection shatters the power of fear. Because Christ is risen we no longer allow fear to dominate, control, or manipulate us. We don't remain imprisoned in the tombs of our past failures or buried under the weight of present anxiety. In the risen Christ old things pass away and everything becomes new.

The Easter earthquake
shakes our assumptions about the world around us.

The stone-moving angel says, "[Jesus] is going ahead of you to Galilee; there you will see him" (Matt. 28:7). Galilee—their old world, the place they left behind when they first followed Jesus. Who wants to go back there? But Christ is already on the way to Galilee, and there they will see him.

The Resurrection unhinges the assumption that this world is something we leave behind. Instead, Easter promises that what God does in the resurrection of Jesus is God's intention for the entire creation. The Resurrection contradicts the assumption that Christ resides on an ethereal cloud in a distant heaven. Rather, we find him on the dusty road that leads to the real stuff of our ordinary world. If our eyes are open to see him, we can find him everywhere!

The Easter earthquake
shakes our assumptions about death.

Matthew leaves no doubt that Jesus was dead. The rock-hewn tomb, the large stone at the door, Pilate's guards, and the seal of the Roman Empire all confirm that fact. It takes nothing less than the infinite power of the Almighty God to shake the earth, break open the tomb, and raise Jesus from the dead.

The gospel never promises that we will escape death. In fact, it says that in spite of our attempts to deny it, we will all die. None of us will get out of here alive. But Charles Wesley expressed the soul-shaking promise in his noted Easter hymn:

Soar we now where Christ has led,
Following our exalted Head.
Made like him, like him we rise,
Ours the cross, the grave, the skies. (UMH, no. 302)

In my sermon on the Easter Sunday after the death of one of my closest friends, I shared the story of the way his toddler grandson would come from his bedroom early in the morning, climb up into his grandfather's lap, and whisper in his ear, "New day, Papa. New day." Because of the Easter earthquake, tomorrow is never just another day. It's as if the angel at the tomb says to all of us every morning, "New day, children. New day!"

The Invitation

New Testament scholar N. T. Wright pointed out in his book *Surprised by Hope* that we sometimes "keep Lent, Holy Week and Good Friday so thoroughly that we have hardly any energy left for Easter." But he declares, "Easter should be the center. Take that away and there is, almost literally, nothing left."[1]

I invite you to place Easter at the center of your Lenten journey. It's the invitation to see the dark, deadly realities of our lives in light of the Resurrection. I invite you to watch for the way the Easter earthquake shifts the ground beneath some of our common assumptions and holds out before us a new way of living.

In the liturgical tradition, Lent involves forty days of spiritual discipline that lead to the cross. In this serious season, we face the dark realities of the sin in our lives and the suffering of the world. But the forty days do not include Sundays. We celebrate Sunday as the day of Resurrection—a weekly reminder that our world's dark realities are the shadow side of the light that shines from an empty tomb. It's the joyful declaration of a new day dawning for us and for our world.

Instead of giving up something for Lent, I invite you to take up a daily discipline of reflection on scripture and prayer. Like the liturgical calendar, we will begin each week with a longer reflection on the Resurrection while drawing on the suggested readings for the daily meditations. It's also the invitation to share our individual discoveries with other disciples in a small group in the assurance that the risen Christ who appeared to the disciples gathered in the upper room will be present among us as well. You will find "A Guide for Small-Group Gatherings" on page 119.

I've included a "Hymn of the Week" that connects with the content of that week's study. I encourage you to find a recording or YouTube video of the hymn and include it in your personal meditation or small-group gathering. Feel free to choose other songs that speak to you for use during this time as well.

One traditional Resurrection hymn calls us to "sing the resurrection song!" (UMH, no. 702). William Marcus James was in his late nineties when I met him. He was born in Mississippi in 1915 and grew up in the dark days of racial segregation. Ordained in The Methodist Church in 1938, he served most of his pastoral ministry in Harlem as a voice for racial justice and nonviolence in New York City and throughout his denomination. He continued to be full of life until he died at ninety-seven. His best-known hymn is a bold declaration of life in the power of the Resurrection.

> Easter people, raise your voices,
> sounds of heaven in earth should ring.
> Christ has brought us heaven's choices;
> heavenly music, let it ring.
> Alleluia! Alleluia!
> Easter people, let us sing.
>
> Fear of death can no more stop us
> from our pressing here below.
> For our Lord empowered us

to triumph over every foe.
Alleluia! Alleluia!
On to victory now we go.

Every day to us is Easter,
with its resurrection song.
When in trouble move the faster
to our God who rights the wrong.
Alleluia! Alleluia!
See the power of heavenly throngs. (UMH, no. 304)

—WILLIAM M. JAMES

Welcome to life in the aftermath of the Easter earthquake!

ASH WEDNESDAY

BEGINNING WHERE OUR STORIES END
Read Matthew 27:57-61; Psalm 51.

Our Lenten journey begins at the place where all our journeys end: the stony silence of a tomb. We begin at Joseph's tomb, the place where Jesus' body was laid to rest.

My favorite place in the Washington National Cathedral is the Chapel of St. Joseph of Arimathea. Deep below the nave, the chapel is formed by the massive piers that support the Gloria in Excelsis Tower that rises three hundred feet above the highest point of land in the District of Columbia. Twelve descending steps create the feeling of descending into the tomb while sensing the full weight and glory of the tower above.

Behind the altar, a mural by Jan Henrik De Rosen depicts Joseph leading the procession to the tomb. The people's heads are shrouded or bowed except for one young man who helps carry the body. He faces directly toward the congregation. Looking into his eyes, I often wonder what he is saying to or asking of us.

On Ash Wednesday, the young man reminds me that we all make this journey. It's the ruthlessly honest word spoken as the ashes are placed on our foreheads, "Remember that you are dust and to dust you will return."

Nothing is quieter than death, nothing more silent than a grave. Lent leads us into that silence. The church invites us to break away from the nonstop chatter of our culture in order to be still long enough to hear God's voice. Our Lenten journey begins with this invitation:

> I invite you, therefore, in the name of the Church,
>> to observe a holy Lent:
>> by self-examination and repentance;
>> by prayer, fasting, and self-denial;
>> and by reading and meditating on God's Holy Word.
> To make a right beginning of repentance,
>> and as a mark of our mortal nature,
>> let us now kneel before our Creator and Redeemer.
>
> (UMBOW, no. 322)

Lent begins at the tomb where we acknowledge our dusty humanity and confess our sin. With the guilt-ridden David in Psalm 51, we name our need for God's mercy, forgiveness, and cleansing. With saints throughout the ages, we cry,

> *Kyrie eleison.*
>> Lord, have mercy.
> *Christe eleison.*
>> Christ, have mercy.

The powerful paradox of Lent is that we make our way to the tomb in the promise of resurrection. We wear the ashes of our mortality in the hope of eternal life. We name our sin and acknowledge our need in the assurance of God's love and grace. Paul expressed that paradox when he wrote these words:

> As dying, and see—we are alive; as punished, and yet not killed; as sorrowful, yet always rejoicing; as poor,

yet making many rich; as having nothing, and yet possessing everything. (2 Cor. 6:9-10)

Like the earthquake in the Gospel, a 5.8-magnitude earthquake shook Washington, DC, on August 23, 2011. As the energy from the quake traveled upward, it shook the highest and most slender elements of the Gloria in Excelsis tower. Delicate pinnacles, each weighing thousands of pounds, burst apart from the seismic force unleashed in less than a minute. Repairs will take more than a decade at an estimated cost of $22 million.

But the tower still stands with its foundation deep in the walls of St. Joseph's chapel. Standing firmly in the place of death, we know the hope and promise of the glory that rises above us.

HYMN OF THE DAY

"Lord, Who Throughout These Forty Days"

Lord, who throughout these forty days
for us didst fast and pray,
teach us with thee to mourn our sins
and close by thee to stay.

As thou with Satan didst contend,
and didst the victory win,
O give us strength in thee to fight,
in thee to conquer sin.

And through these days of penitence,
and through thy passiontide,
yea, evermore in life and death,
Jesus, with us abide.

Abide with us, that so,
this life of suffering over past,
an Easter of unending joy
we may attain at last. (UMH, no. 269)

—Claudia F. Herneman

SUGGESTIONS FOR SMALL-GROUP INTERACTION

❖ Invite group members to share their experience of Ash Wednesday.

❖ Show a picture of the Chapel of St. Joseph of Arimathea. What do they observe? What feelings does the art generate within them?

❖ Attend an Ash Wednesday service together.

FIRST WEEK IN LENT

∞

SHAKING THE POWERS

Trembling and shaking the earth pointed to another ground on which the earth itself rests: the self-surrendering love on which all earthly powers and values concentrate their hostility and which they cannot conquer.

—Paul Tillich

SUNDAY

SHAKING THE TOMB
Read Matthew 27:62-66.

Go," Pilate told the guards, "make it as secure as you can." Talk about a boring assignment! Guarding a grave had to be as exciting as watching paint dry. But they followed Pilate's orders. They put the seal of Roman authority on the tomb. You couldn't get more secure than that.

"Go, make it as secure as you can" is the last word we hear from Pilate and the worst word that the powers of evil, injustice, suffering, and death can speak. It sends a clear message: Rome is in charge here! Silence Jesus' subversive teaching. Shut down his disruptive movement. Seal the door. Make it as secure as possible.

But the worst word is not the last word. God gets the last word with the sound of an earthquake. Only the Gospel of Matthew even attempts to describe that moment. In the sixteenth century, Matthias Grünewald tried to paint it in the Resurrection panel of the Isenheim Altarpiece.

Looking at Grünewald's painting, you can feel the earth's vibration and hear the earthquake's rumble. The grave is broken open. The guards tumble to the ground. The risen Christ soars out of the grave. Jesus' face dissolves into the brilliant sun that penetrates the darkness. He raises his nail-scarred hands as if to say, "Be not afraid! I am going before you!" It is Grünewald's visual expression of Resurrection power that shakes not only the earth but the powers of evil, sin, and death.

In Matthew's account, no one sees or meets Jesus at the tomb. The angel tells the women, "Go quickly and tell his disciples, 'He has been raised from the dead, and indeed he is going ahead of you to Galilee; there you will see him'" (28:7).

The women begin running down the road, and then Matthew tells us, "Jesus met them." He repeats the command, "Go and tell my brothers to go to Galilee; there they will see me" (28:10).

Pilate's command to the guards: "Go, make it as secure as you can." The angel's command to the women: "Go quickly and tell his disciples, 'He has been raised from the dead.'" One command declares the power of death; the other announces the power of new life. One represents the political powers of this world; the other represents the power of God. Pilate plays "Taps"; the angel plays "Reveille."

We are easily tempted to believe that the angel said, "He has been raised and is going into heaven where you will see him when you die." That represents the way we sometimes live. We celebrate the Resurrection as a past event, and we look forward to a resurrection after death—but in between, we live as if Jesus has left us to muddle through life on our own. But that's not what Matthew says. The angel tells the women that Jesus goes ahead of them into a very real, this-worldly place called Galilee, and there they will see him.

The point of the Resurrection is not that Jesus has gone to heaven and if we stay faithful for the rest of our lives, we will see him there after we die. The promise is not simply a new life that awaits us after death but a new life that begins right now, and death can never defeat it. We live now in ways that bear witness to the way this world will be when God's kingdom comes and God's will is done on earth as it is already done in heaven. In the aftermath of the Easter earthquake, we live now in the power of the risen Christ.

PRAYER FOCUS

- ❖ How and where have you experienced the powers of evil, injustice, and death?
- ❖ What does it mean for you to hear the command, "Go, tell his disciples he has been raised from the dead"?

HYMN OF THE WEEK

"The Strife Is O'er"

The strife is o'er, the battle done;
the victory of life is won;
the song of triumph has begun:
Alleluia!

The powers of death have done their worst,
but Christ their legions hath dispersed;
let shouts of holy joy outburst:
Alleluia!

Lord, by the stripes which wounded thee,
from death's dread sting thy servants free,
that we may live, and sing to thee:
Alleluia! (UMH, no. 306)

> —Anon. Latin, translated by Francis Pott

MONDAY

THE VOICE THAT SHAKES THE WILDERNESS
Read Psalm 29; Mark 1:9-11.

I've never experienced an earthquake, but I have been through a hurricane. My wife and I watched it make its way across the Atlantic and into the Gulf of Mexico. We felt an eerie silence as we packed our car and left our home behind when the evacuation order came. We watched the sky turn a dark, ominous gray and listened as the wind and rain whirled around us. We gave a sigh of relief when the storm passed and we were safe at home again.

The power of a hurricane animates my reading of Psalm 29. It appears in the suggested reading for the Sunday on which we remember Jesus' baptism because of its description of the voice that speaks over the waters (29:3). It is the visual reminder that the God whose Spirit descended on Jesus like a dove is the same God whose power breaks trees, unleashes flames, convulses oaks, and shakes the wilderness.

Immediately after the baptism, Mark uses a strong Greek verb to say that the Spirit "drove him out into the wilderness" (Mark 1:12). Jesus does not choose to go to the wilderness; the Spirit compels him to go.

Throughout scripture, the wilderness represents more than a lonely, barren place on the map. It's the place where God's people confront the ruthless power of temptation; where they wrestle with questions about who they are, where they are going, and how they are going to get there. It's where Jesus faces the temptations to deny his identity as the Son of God, to use divine power to satisfy his human desires, to find a less costly way of doing the expensive work of salvation.

For all disciples, the wilderness is the barren space between where we've been and where we're going. It's the empty place between a familiar, comfortable past and an unfamiliar, often risky, future. It's the soul-searching place where we face the temptations to settle for things that are less than God's best for us, to take a shortcut to get to Easter without going through Lent, to experience new life without going to the cross.

In the wilderness of our own souls, everything else is torn away; we find ourselves naked and vulnerable in the presence of God, whose Spirit descends like a dove and shakes the earth.

PRAYER FOCUS

❖ When have you experienced God's Spirit shaking the wilderness?

❖ What constitutes the wilderness in your life?

TUESDAY

WRESTLING WILD BEASTS WITH JESUS
Read Mark 1:12-13; Hebrews 4:14-16.

Mark's account of Jesus' time in the wilderness reminds me of the children's book by Maurice Sendak: *Where the Wild Things Are*. It tells the story of Max, who made so much mischief that his mother called him "Wild Thing" and sent him to bed without his supper.

That night, Max sailed away to the place where the wild things "roared their terrible roars and gnashed their terrible teeth and rolled their terrible eyes and showed their terrible claws." But Max stared "into all their yellow eyes without blinking once and they were frightened and called him the most wild thing of all." In the end, Max sailed back to "his very own room where he found his supper waiting for him and it was still hot."[1]

Mark is the only Gospel writer who says that Jesus was "with the wild beasts." He might have meant actual animals, but it could also be his metaphorical description of "wild beasts" of temptation. Even the Son of God could not fulfill God's purpose for his life until he faced the power of temptation.

Matthew and Luke itemize the details of Jesus' temptations and portray the way Jesus looks them in the eyes without blinking and defeats them. But Mark doesn't name the temptations. Perhaps he wants us to identify the deeply personal temptations with which we wrestle in the wilderness of our own souls. Here is John Wesley's description of that struggle:

> Self-will, which suffers not Christ to reign over us, self-righteousness, which renounces the righteousness of God, our Saviour, and our own fleshly wisdom . . . are undoubtedly the great enemies we have to contend with, and assault us in a thousand shapes. But I find . . . self-will to be the hardest of all to conquer.[2]

In whatever way we name the wild beasts, the writer of Hebrews offers a word of encouragement:

> We do not have a high priest who is unable to sympathize with our weaknesses, but we have one who in every respect has been tested as we are, yet without sin. Let us therefore approach the throne of grace with boldness, so that we may receive mercy and find grace to help in time of need. (4:15-16)

We do not enter the wilderness alone. We go with the presence of the One who has been there before us, the One who gives mercy and grace for our time of need.

Mark says that after Jesus' temptation, "angels waited on him." It reminds me of the psalmist's saying, "You prepare a table before me in the presence of my enemies" (Ps. 23:5). In the end, we return to the table of our Lord where we know we are loved and discover that God's presence is there to strengthen us.

PRAYER FOCUS

❖ What "wild beasts" do you face in your life?

❖ Will you claim the promise that Jesus faces them with you?

WEDNESDAY

TO HELL WITH JESUS
Read 1 Peter 3:18-22.

I've never used the title of today's reflection for a sermon, though I considered it every time I preached on the clause of the Apostles' Creed that says, "He descended into hell." A younger, less-restrained pastor used it as the title of his ordination sermon. He told his story of how Christ descended into the hell of his life. Everything had fallen apart around him like poorly constructed buildings collapsing during an earthquake. His addiction to alcohol and drugs had landed him in prison.

But the risen Christ descended into the hell this man had made of his life, brought new light into the darkness and new hope into his despair. He stands as a living witness to the life-giving power of the risen Christ who suffered for our sins, was put to death in the flesh and made alive in the Spirit, and who came down to proclaim good news "to the spirits in prison."

"He descended into hell" doesn't appear in some versions of the creed because of a debate in the early church about where

Jesus was hanging out from Good Friday night until Easter morning. Saint Augustine (354–430 CE) taught that Jesus literally descended into hell to take the gospel to the spirits there. But even he admitted uncertainty about it. The Protestant reformers left it out because today's reading is the only somewhat-vague reference to it in scripture and because it was linked to the Roman Catholic understanding of purgatory.

But like my young clergy friend, a hospital chaplain stated that patients in the psychiatric ward insisted that this clause be included in their worship because it affirmed that Christ had descended into the hell they experienced. One of Charles Wesley's best-loved hymns expresses it this way:

He left His Father's throne above
(so free, so infinite his grace!),
emptied himself of all but love,
and bled for Adam's helpless race:
'Tis mercy all, immense and free,
For O my God, it found out me!

Long my imprisoned spirit lay,
fast bound in sin and nature's night;
thine eye diffused a quickening ray;
I woke, the dungeon flamed with light;
my chains fell off, my heart was free,
I rose, went forth, and followed thee. (UMH, no. 363)

PRAYER FOCUS

❖ What difference does it make for you to know that the risen Christ "descended into hell"?

❖ When have you known the presence of the One who left his Father's throne, emptied himself of all but love, and entered into your life?

THURSDAY

THE ONES FOR WHOM THE WORLD WAITS

Read Genesis 9:8-17; Romans 8:18-25.

Why does Noah's story show up in the scripture readings during Lent? The textual link is yesterday's reading, which makes a direct comparison between the ark and our baptism. (See 1 Peter 3:20.) But it still seems like an odd story to tell on the way to Easter.

Looking more closely, however, we can see that the reading is not about Noah but about God. It's the bold announcement of God's gracious, unilateral, self-binding covenant with the whole creation. God hangs the bow in the sky as the irrevocable reminder of "the everlasting covenant between God and every living creature of all flesh that is on the earth." God intends not the destruction but the salvation of the entire cosmos.

God's covenant with creation stands in stark contrast to Thomas L. Friedman's experience with eight thousand scientists, nature reserve specialists, and environmentalists who are part of the International Union for Conservation of Nature. He notes in his article "We Are All Noah Now," his *New York Times* op-ed piece (September 7, 2016) that our natural world is rapidly disappearing. We are "bumping up against and piercing planetary boundaries . . . from which Mother Nature will not be able to recover." One ambassador stated, "Deeply, desperately, we are hoping someone will do something before it is too late. That someone we are hoping for is you."

Friedman could have been channeling the apostle Paul who wrote, "The creation waits with eager longing for the revealing of the children of God" (Rom. 8:19).

Perhaps one of the most insidious temptations we face is to believe that salvation is all about us, that the purpose of God's amazing work of grace in the death and resurrection of Jesus is only for individual human souls. In fact, God's saving purpose encompasses the whole creation, and we are called to participate in that salvation.

Prayer Focus

❖ How does God's covenant with Noah speak to you?

❖ How will you become one for whom creation waits?

Friday

For Spacious Skies
Read Psalm 118.

The skies were not spacious over Washington, DC, on July 4. The fireworks were muted by heavy, grey clouds that hung like a wet blanket over the Mall. By contrast, the sky was cloudlessly clear, and the sun was peeking over the horizon when I made my way onto the running trail that winds along the outskirts of Sioux Falls, South Dakota. In awe of the "spacious skies" and "amber waves of grain" that stretched out as far as I could see, I remembered the psalmist's words: "In tight circumstances, I cried out to the Lord. The Lord answered me with wide-open spaces" (Ps. 118:5, CEB) A Hebrew scholar told me that the word *merhab* means "vast expanse" or "broad place." It refers to "Yahweh's celestial abode"; in other words, "spacious skies." It can also mean "salvation." It appears again in 2 Samuel 22:20 and Psalms 18:19; 31:8; 119:45.

Caught up in the sheer immensity of the earth and sky that morning, I experienced the presence of God, whose power shakes the earth. It reminded me that God's salvation is cosmic in scale.

I grew up believing that salvation was something that happened after the altar call during the singing of "Just as I Am," when someone prayed for God's forgiveness and accepted Christ into their lives. I still believe that experience can be part of God's work of salvation. But there is more.

Salvation is an ongoing work of grace through which I am being released from the suffocating smallness of life turned in on itself to live in the spacious greatness of God's boundless life and love. I'm being set free from the "tight circumstances" of a rigid legalism that needs to squeeze everyone else into my narrow assumptions so I can experience expansive receptivity to others. I am being healed from the sin of selfishness in order to live in the infinite unselfishness of God. I am being saved from a life motivated by self-serving so I can experience the self-giving life of Jesus Christ. I am being stretched to participate in God's salvation that reaches to the whole creation.

Thanks be to God for the spacious skies of saving grace, unending love, and relentless hope!

PRAYER FOCUS

❖ Where are the "tight" places in your life?

❖ How is God's grace opening you to the "spacious skies" of God's infinite love?

SUGGESTIONS FOR SMALL-GROUP INTERACTION

❖ Invite group members to share their wilderness experiences.

❖ How do they feel about the clause in the creed that says Jesus "descended into hell"?

❖ What do group members see as their part in caring for creation?

∞

SURPRISING HOPE

We live our lives in the practice of what we do not originate and cannot anticipate. When we practice resurrection, we continuously enter into what is more than we are. When we practice resurrection, we keep company with Jesus, alive and present.

—Eugene H. Peterson

SUNDAY

SURPRISE!
Read Mark 16:1-8.

I often remind my brother who lives in California that the difference between earthquakes and hurricanes is that we Floridians know when a hurricane is coming. We track it from the time it forms off the coast of Africa until it roars along the coast of Florida. An earthquake, on the other hand, comes by surprise—just the way the earth shook on Good Friday afternoon and Easter Sunday morning.

A preacher friend told the story of a father who took his young daughter shopping for an Easter dress. Walking through the mall, the daughter said, "I can't wait for Easter!" Wanting to be sure she knew that Easter was more than a spring fashion show, her father asked, "Do you know what Easter means?" The little girl threw her arms up in the air and shouted, "Surprise!"

Each Gospel offers its unique version of what happened on Easter morning, but they have two aspects in common. They agree that the women are the first people to experience the empty tomb. And they agree that it comes as a surprise. No one expected a resurrection.

These are, after all, the same women who watched the whole ghastly ordeal on Friday afternoon. They heard Jesus take his last breath. They saw Joseph pull his bloody body down from the cross, wrap it in a linen cloth, and lay it in the tomb. They heard the heartrending thud as the stone rolled against the opening. All they expected to find at the tomb was a rigid, lifeless corpse. Their only question was, "Who will roll away the stone for us?"

But something happened that morning that surprised the living daylights out of them and shook the assumptions upon which they lived. "When they looked up, they saw that the stone, which was very large, had already been rolled back" (Mark 16:4). The Resurrection had already happened. In the place where they expected to find death, they heard the unexpected announcement, "He has been raised"—short enough to post on Twitter but big enough to change the world.

Don't miss Mark's use of the passive voice. God acted on behalf of the dead Jesus in the Resurrection; Jesus could not do this for himself. God confirms that the life and death of Jesus is the way God intends to save, redeem, and restore our sin-broken lives and the whole sin-damaged creation.

The Resurrection means that we no longer need to settle for this old world the way it has been. The same power that raised Jesus from the dead can energize us to be part of this world's becoming what God intends it to be. Evil, injustice, suffering, and death may have their day, but the victory has already been won in the risen Christ.

In his oil painting titled *The Chess Players* (also known as *Checkmate*), Friedrich August Moritz Retzsch (1779–1857) offered his artistic interpretation of the legend of Faust, who gambled his soul with the devil and lost. Faust stares at the chess board in abject despair. The devil leers in eager anticipation of victory. An angel in the background looks down with pity on Faust's position.

That was everyone's understanding of the painting until 1889 when chess master Paul Morphy studied the painting and said, "I think I can take the young man's game and win." According to the *Columbia Chess Chronicle*, published in the fall of 1888, "To the surprise of every one, victory was snatched from the devil and the young man saved."

That's the earthshaking surprise of Easter! To everyone's surprise, when it looked as if evil, injustice, sin, and death had won, God had another move. No wonder these women are astonished. What they expect to be the end of Jesus' story is just the beginning of a story that never ends. What a surprise!

PRAYER FOCUS

❖ In what ways do you identify with the women as they come to the tomb?

❖ How have you experienced the surprise of God's victory in your own life?

Hymn of the Week

"Christ Jesus Lay in Death's Strong Bands"

Christ Jesus lay in death's strong bands,
for our offenses given;
but now at God's right hand he stands,
and brings us life from heaven;
wherefore let us joyful be,
and sing to God right thankfully
loud songs of Alleluia!
Alleluia!

It was a strange and dreadful strife
when life and death contended;
the victory remained with life;
the reign of death was ended.
Stripped of power, no more it reigns,
an empty form alone remains;
death's sting is lost forever!
Alleluia!

So let us keep the festival
whereto the Lord invites us;
Christ is himself the joy of all,
the Sun that warms and lights us.
By his grace he doth impart
eternal sunshine to the heart;
the night of sin is ended!
Alleluia! (UMH, no. 319)

—Martin Luther

MONDAY

SARAH'S SURPRISE
Read Genesis 17:1-7, 15-16.

I've never been able to improve on Frederick Buechner's interpretation of today's scripture reading.

> The place to start is with a woman laughing. . . . She hunches her shoulders around her ears and starts to shake. . . . her laughter is all China teeth and wheeze and tears running down as she rocks back and forth in her kitchen chair. She is laughing because she is pushing ninety-one hard and has just been told she is going to have a baby. . . . She can't control herself, and her husband can't control himself either. He keeps a straight face a few seconds longer than she does, but he ends by cracking up, too. . . .
>
> They are laughing at the idea of a baby's being born in the geriatric ward and Medicare's picking up the tab. They are laughing because the angel not only seems to believe it but seems to expect them to believe it too. . . . They are laughing because if by some crazy chance it should just happen to come true, then they would really have something to laugh about.[1]

We first hear the laughter of disbelief that says, "You've got to be kidding!" It's the skeptical laughter we try to hide when we are around church people who appear to be absolutely sure of everything. But it's still there, percolating inside, waiting for an appropriate time and place to name the doubt and share the skepticism. It is the half-believing laughter of a promise we hope will one day be fulfilled in spite of the odds against it.

Sarah and Abraham, of course, get the last laugh when the baby is born. They name him Isaac, which means "laughter." Sarah says, "God has brought laughter for me; everyone who hears will laugh with me" (Gen. 21:6).

None of the women is laughing on her way to the tomb. The surprise they discovered left them shaking in fear. The disciples laughed at the women because they thought it was "an idle tale" (Luke 24:11). It was more than they could believe. But I like to imagine that gathered around the dinner table with the risen Christ in the upper room (Luke 24:36-43), they found themselves laughing with the deep, life-giving, hope-bringing laughter of God—who always gets the last laugh.

PRAYER FOCUS

❖ When have you shared with others the laughter of disbelief?

❖ What doubts do you bring to your reading of the Gospels?

TUESDAY

HOPING AGAINST HOPE
Read Romans 4:13-25.

Do you ever doubt the message of the cross and the reality of resurrection? Do you wonder if God's promises will ever come true?

After Isaac's birth, I suspect Abraham would have confessed that sometimes he wondered if the promise would ever be fulfilled. So many things were stacked against it: "his own body, which was already as good as dead . . . the barrenness of Sarah's womb" (Rom, 4:19), the sheer passage of time. By all human standards, the chances of having a child were nil. But Paul wrote,

"No distrust made him waver concerning the promise of God."
Instead, Abraham "grew strong in his faith . . . fully convinced
that God was able to do what he had promised" (Rom. 4:19-21)

Alfred Lord Tennyson described the same journey of faith
in the life of his friend Arthur Henry Hallam in his poem "In
Memoriam":

> Perplext in faith, but pure in deeds,
>> At last he beat his music out.
>> There lives more faith in honest doubt,
> Believe me, than in half the creeds.
>
> He fought his doubts and gather'd strength,
>> He would not make his judgment blind,
>> He faced the specters of the mind
> And laid them: thus he came at length
>
> To find a stronger faith his own;
>> And Power was with him in the night,
>> Which makes the darkness and the light,
> And dwells not in the light alone.

Along the way through Lent to Easter, we may question how
this story relates to us. When we face the awful reality of death,
it can be difficult to believe in the promise of resurrection. When
we see the suffering, injustice, and pain in our world, hope can
sometimes give way to despair. We may start thinking that the
hope for new life is "an idle tale" (Luke 24:11).

But Abraham's witness encourages us to grow stronger
in faith as we dare to believe that what God did in the death
and resurrection of Jesus is God's way of winning the ultimate
victory over suffering, pain, and death. As we work through
our questions and doubts, we can "find a stronger faith" and

experience the presence of God "which makes the darkness and the light" that is not found "in the light alone."

Prayer Focus

❖ When have you doubted God's promise in your life or for the world?

❖ Where have you seen evidence that God can do what God has promised?

Wednesday

The Surprising Paradox
Read Mark 8:31-38.

It was a cold, clear day in Florida. Accustomed to shuttle launches, I no longer watched every time one lifted off from the Cape. Suddenly a woman dashed into my office. With tears running down her cheeks, she said, "The shuttle just exploded!" We rushed outside and stared speechless at the white streak that began on the horizon, arose in a perfect arc, and then stopped abruptly. It lingered as a mute witness to an immense tragedy.

Two hours later a NASA official called. The finalists in the "Teacher in Space" program were coming to a nearby hotel and they wanted a pastor to meet them. I got to the hotel to discover an exceptionally ordinary group of people: a social studies teacher from Houston, an astronomy teacher from New England, an elementary school teacher from Kentucky. I listened to their stories, felt their grief and loss. But I remember the strength of their determination that the program go on. If given the opportunity, they were ready to go themselves.

I feel that same unyielding determination when I hear Jesus say, "The Son of Man *must* undergo great suffering, and be rejected . . . and be killed, and after three days rise again" (Mark 8:31, italics added). Having met those teachers, I heard Jesus' words with different ears: "If any want to become my followers, let them deny themselves and take up their cross and follow me. For those who want to save their life will lose it, and those who lose their life for my sake, and for the sake of the gospel, will save it" (Mark 8:34-35).

The surprising paradox of the gospel is that real life is not found in self-aggrandizement but in self-surrender; not in protecting ourselves but in giving ourselves away; not by holding our lives tightly but by being held by a relentless love that is stronger than our own.

M. Scott Peck wrote the following: "The tentacles of narcissism are subtle and penetrating and must be hacked away one by one, day after day, week after week, month after month, year after year." Peck also discovered that

> the further we proceed in diminishing our narcissism—
> our self-centeredness and sense of self-importance—
> the more we discover ourselves becoming not only
> less fearful of death, but also less fearful of life.
> . . . We begin to experience a sustained kind of
> happiness we never experienced before, as we become
> more self-forgetful and hence progressively more able to
> remember God.[2]

PRAYER FOCUS

❖ How have "the tentacles of narcissism" penetrated your life?

❖ What will it mean for you to surrender your self-centeredness to the infinite love of God?

THURSDAY

SURPRISED BY GOD
Read Mark 9:2-9; 2 Peter 1:16-19.

The disciples really were surprised! I figure that when they headed for the hills that day they thought they were going for exercise. They never expected an extraordinary experience of God's presence. They stand speechless, except for Peter who stated what they all must have felt: "It feels so good to be here! Let's put up tents and stay!" (AP) But as suddenly as the vision came, it disappeared. They were left with nothing but Jesus and with the memory of that moment to sustain their faith across the years ahead.

Sometimes the Spirit leads us to a mountaintop where we catch a glimpse of God's glory and know with unquestioned assurance that the one we follow is the Son of God. Now and then we experience Christ robed in dazzling white and feel the presence of saints who have gone before us. Along the pathway of discipleship, we encounter wonder-filled moments of spiritual awareness that revolutionize our lives and transfigure the way we see the world around us. Like Peter, we desperately long to take up residence in that place or to hold on to it forever. We may be tempted to expect every moment of our life to be filled with an extraordinary sense of glory, assurance, and peace.

But then we come down from the mountain and walk through the world where Jesus walked and where the risen Christ promised to meet us. Most of the time our path leads through ordinary places in an ordinary world filled with ordinary people who experience ordinary hurts, frustrations, fears, and doubts. Most days we simply follow Jesus in the way of humble, self-emptying servanthood. Like the disciples, we are left with "only

Jesus," who reveals the surprising way in which God's kingdom comes and God's will is done in this world.

In the book of Revelation, John glimpses spectacular scenes of heavenly worship that resemble the Transfiguration—but on steroids: Saints robed in dazzling white sing praises in the fully revealed presence of God. In one scene, John names those saints as those who "follow the Lamb wherever he goes" (Rev. 14:4).

In life, in death, and in life beyond death, we follow Jesus wherever he goes.

PRAYER FOCUS

❖ When have you glimpsed God's glory?

❖ How have transfiguring experiences sustained you as you live out ordinary days?

FRIDAY

MY GOD, WHY?
Read Psalm 22.

If Neil Armstrong's "one small step for man" was also one giant leap for humankind, that's also what we see in the gigantic leap from the mountain of Transfiguration to the hill called Calvary.

Who would have predicted that the man who stood on the mountain robed in dazzling white would be the man hanging naked on a cross? Who could have anticipated that the one of whom the voice in the cloud declared, "This is my Son, the Beloved" (Matt. 3:17) would be the one gasping, "My God, my God, why have you forsaken me?" (Ps. 22:1).

The psalm confirms that Jesus was not the first person to ask that question. Nor was he the last. Sooner or later, every one of us will ask it. But this isn't just anyone; this mangled man on the cross is the Son of God! The Nicene Creed affirms him as "God from God, Light from Light, true God from true God" (UMH, no. 880). No wonder the sun turned dark, the earth shook, and rocks split open. No wonder the mocking crowd said, "If you are the Son of God, come down from the cross" (Matt. 27:40).

Those in the mocking crowd did not understand that Jesus' very identity as the Son of God (the human expression of God's self-giving love) meant that he could not save *himself* and be the Son who saves *us*. The Incarnation means that the moment Jesus felt most forsaken by God was the same moment that God was deeply present with all of us.

In his novel, *The Shack*, William Paul Young imagined a moment when Mack, the central character in the story, notices the scars on God's wrists, and the character representing God says, "Don't ever think that what my son chose to do didn't cost us dearly. Love always leaves a significant mark. . . . We were there *together*."[3] The mind-blowing surprise of the gospel is that "God was reconciling the world to himself through Christ" (2 Cor. 5:19, CEB) when Jesus was hanging on the cross.

Matthew records that when the centurion and his fellow guards felt the earth shake and heard Jesus utter his final words, they said, "Truly this man was God's Son!" (Matt. 27:54).

It really was one small step for a human, but a gigantic leap for all humankind.

PRAYER FOCUS

❖ When have you felt forsaken by God?

❖ What difference will it make for you to believe that God was present with us at the cross?

SUGGESTIONS FOR SMALL-GROUP INTERACTION

❖ Find a copy of Retzsch's painting of *The Chess Players* and spend time in silence with the painting.

❖ Invite group members to share their observations about the painting. What do they see? How does it make them feel?

❖ Ask members to tell the group about their "mountaintop" experiences.

❖ Invite members to share their experiences of feeling forsaken by God.

∞

BEYOND BELIEF

The final step on the way to holiness in Christ is then to completely abandon ourselves with confident joy to the apparent madness of the cross. . . . It is a twisting, a letting go, an act of total abandonment. But it is also a final break-through into joy.

—Thomas Merton

SUNDAY

DANCING WITH THE SUN
Read Psalm 19:1-6.

My favorite contemporary Easter song "Was It a Morning Like This?" raises the question: "Did the grass sing?/ Did the earth rejoice to feel you again?" Might the earthquake at the tomb be the earth itself reverberating with the joy of resurrection? On Easter morning, does the whole universe join in singing "Christ the Lord Is Risen Today"?

In the seventeenth century, faithful people in Ireland would get up before dawn and make their way to a hilltop. There they would wait to see the sun dance a jig as it rose on Easter morning. English poet, John Suckling (1609–41), used that tradition to describe a bride on her wedding day in his poem "A Ballad upon a Wedding."

> But oh! she dances such a way
> > No sun upon an Easter-day
> > Is half so fine a sight.

The Gospels don't describe the sun dancing on Easter morning, but the writer of Psalm 19 does say that the heavens—the entire solar system and countless unnamed galaxies—declare the glory of God. The psalmist compares the sun to a bridegroom dancing at his wedding. The writer of Psalm 65 hears "the gateways of the morning and the evening shout for joy" and the meadows and valleys "shout and sing together for joy" (Ps. 65:8, 13). Isaiah announces the promise that "the mountains and the hills before you shall burst into song, and all the trees of the field shall clap their hands" (Isa. 55:12). Can we believe that this is more than metaphor? Could it be that the entire universe feels the effects of God's presence? Is God's work through the death and resurrection of Jesus not only for individual human beings but for the whole creation?

If your spiritual roots were planted in the same theological soil as mine, you grew up believing that the purpose of the Christian faith was to ensure that people had "fire insurance" against going to hell and were headed to heaven. I was taught to ask, "If you died tonight and God asked you, 'Why should I let you into my heaven?' what would you say?" Giving the right answer to that question was all-important.

But as I matured in my faith, dug deeper into scripture, and experienced a larger world than the one in which I grew up, that definition of salvation began to feel quite small. I sensed that the Bible proclaimed a more expansive vision. New Testament scholar N. T. Wright confirmed what I instinctively believed.

> God will redeem the whole universe; Jesus's resurrection is the beginning of that new life, the fresh grass growing through the concrete of corruption and decay in the old world. That final redemption will be the moment when heaven and earth are joined together at last, in a burst of God's creative energy for which Easter is the prototype and source.[1]

The word *Easter* comes from a Latin root meaning "spring." It led the eighth-century theologian and poet, John of Damascus, to write these words:

> 'Tis the spring of souls today;
> Christ hath burst his prison,
> and from three days' sleep in death
> as a sun hath risen;
> all the winter of our sins,
> long and dark, is flying.

C. S. Lewis used a similar image when he described Narnia under the reign of the White Witch as a frigid place where it was always winter but never Christmas. The sign that Aslan (the Christ figure) was on the move came when the snow began to melt, the ice began to thaw, patches of green grass began to appear, and birds began chirping in the trees. The Dwarf warns the witch, "This is no thaw. . . . This is spring. . . . Your winter has been destroyed!"[2]

The sun dancing and the earth singing may stretch our imagination, but what God accomplished in the life, death, and resurrection of Jesus is bigger than anything we can imagine. It includes the renewal and redemption of the whole created order. God's work of salvation is beyond belief!

PRAYER FOCUS

❖ When have you experienced heaven and earth declaring the glory of God?

❖ How does it feel to compare the Resurrection to the coming of spring?

HYMN OF THE WEEK

"Come, Ye Faithful, Raise the Strain"

Come, ye faithful, raise the strain of triumphant gladness;
God hath brought forth Israel into joy from sadness;
loosed from Pharaoh's bitter yoke Jacob's sons and daughters,
led them with unmoistened foot through the Red Sea waters.

'Tis the spring of souls today; Christ hath burst his prison,
and from three days' sleep in death as a sun hath risen;
all the winter of our sins, long and dark, is flying
from his light, to whom we give laud and praise undying.

Now the queen of seasons, bright with the day of splendor,
with the royal feast of feasts, comes its joy to render;
comes to glad Jerusalem, who with true affection
welcomes in unwearied strains Jesus' resurrection.

"Alleluia!" now we cry to our King immortal,
who, triumphant, burst the bars of the tomb's dark portal;
"Alleluia!" with the Son, God the Father praising,
"Alleluia!" yet again to the Spirit raising. (UMH, no. 315)

—John of Damascus

Monday

Finding Jesus
Read Luke 24:13-35.

Two shell-shocked disciples walk from Jerusalem to Emmaus on Sunday afternoon. They feel shaken to the core by their experience. They felt the earth shake at the cross, and now they have heard about an earthquake at the empty tomb. They are stunned with grief, paralyzed by fear, baffled by everything they have seen and heard—the cross too horrible to deny, the Resurrection too good to believe.

The two are so absorbed in their conversation that they don't notice the stranger who walks along beside them. And isn't it just like Jesus to enter gently into their grief, to walk quietly with them through "the valley of the shadow of death" (Ps. 23:4, KJV).

What we need most in times of grief is someone to hear our pain and listen to our story. Jesus listens. Then he helps them see their experience in the broader perspective of God's saving work in scripture.

When the men arrive in Emmaus, Jesus doesn't force himself on them. But when they offer the dinner invitation, "he went in to stay with them." Revelation provides a similar picture when Christ says, "I am standing at the door, knocking; if you hear my voice and open the door, I will come in to you and eat with you, and you with me" (Rev. 3:20). Christ comes, not with a battering ram but with a gentle knock on the door and waits for us to welcome him in.

At their table, Jesus "took bread, blessed and broke it, and gave it to them." With those words, an ordinary supper becomes a sacramental meal in which they recognize Jesus for who he is. They run back to Jerusalem to report that the risen Christ "had been made known to them in the breaking of the bread." While beyond belief, its reality leaves their hearts burning. Charles Wesley captured the mystery when he wrote these words:

> O the depth of love divine,
> the unfathomable grace!
> Who shall say how bread and wine
> God into us conveys!
> How the bread his flesh imparts,
> how the wine transmits his blood,
> fills his faithful people's hearts
> with all the life of God!
>
> Sure and real is the grace,
> the manner be unknown;
> only meet us in thy ways
> and perfect us in one.
> Let us taste the heavenly powers,
> Lord, we ask for nothing more.
> Thine to bless, 'tis only ours
> to wonder and adore.

PRAYER FOCUS

❖ When have you felt the grief, confusion, or fear these disciples must have felt?

❖ How have you experienced the presence of Christ in Holy Communion?

Tuesday

Shaking the Mountain
Read Exodus 20:1-17.

Why read the Ten Commandments during Lent? What does this scripture have to do with God's grace revealed in the death and resurrection of Jesus?

We begin with the backstory in the first nineteen chapters of Exodus. The problem with posting the Ten Commandments in public places is that we then lift them out of the earthshaking setting in which they were given. These are not arbitrary laws that we can separate from the God who gave them.

The story begins with the Israelites in slavery in Egypt. God hears their cries, sends Moses; the rest forms the Bible's primal story of liberation. Three months have passed since Moses led the people out of Egypt and through the Red Sea. The people gather at Mount Sinai, a mountain surrounded with thick clouds and wrapped in smoke. They see lightning, feel thunder, and hear the blast of trumpet as God descends in fire and "the whole mountain [shakes] violently" (Exod. 19:18, CEB). Steven Spielberg could not improve on it!

When God speaks, God reminds the people, "I am the LORD your God, who brought you out of the land of Egypt, out of the house of slavery" (Exod. 20:2).

The God whose presence shakes the mountain is the God who heard their cries when they were in slavery. The God who gives the commandments is the God who freed them from bondage and rescued them when they stood helpless beside the Red Sea. This is the God who, in an amazing act of unexpected grace, saves them when they find themselves utterly incapable of saving themselves.

God doesn't wait for the Israelites to get their act together before saving them; God saves them so they can begin to live in a new way. The God who liberated them now calls them into a unique community that will be defined by their undivided loyalty to God and by these commandments.

Hearing this story in Lent invites us to remember that we too have been in bondage, helplessly held in the power of sin; the love of God in Christ has set us free. "When we were utterly helpless, Christ came at just the right time and died for us sinners" (Rom. 5:6, NLT). God calls us to undivided loyalty to the One who gave himself for us. We are to live into his likeness.

The story that begins at Mount Sinai leads directly to the hill on which Jesus dies. It's beyond belief.

PRAYER FOCUS

❖ How have you experienced God's liberating grace?

❖ What does it mean for you to live into the likeness of God's love?

WEDNESDAY

SHAKING THE TEMPLE
Read John 2:13-22.

All four Gospels record the story of Jesus cleansing the Temple, but none intends it as a ban on bake sales or a justification of human anger. We could view the event as the dramatic fulfillment of the prophetic words that Handel set to music in *Messiah*. A bold bass voice declares, "Yet once a little while and I will shake the heavens and the earth, the sea and the dry land. . . . The Lord, whom ye seek, shall suddenly come to His temple." Then comes the fearful question, "But who may abide the day of His coming, and who shall stand when He appeareth? For He is like a refiner's fire." The full chorus responds, "He shall purify the sons of Levi, that they may offer unto the Lord an offering in righteousness" (based on Haggai 2:6-7; Malachi 3:1-3, KJV).

Jesus shakes the Temple as a God-centered protest against abuse and exploitation. He comes in the spirit of Jeremiah who also calls the Temple "a den of robbers" (7:11) and demands moral and ethical reform. (Read Jeremiah 7:1-15.) He comes not to destroy the religious tradition but to purify it. He comes not in blazing anger but in burning love. He shakes things up because of his all-consuming passion for God's house to be all that God intends it to be. (See Psalm 69:9.) On the cross, he offers his own body so that the refining fire of love and grace may purify God's children.

Jesus still disrupts the patterns of injustice, selfishness, exploitation, and greed that pollute human relationships, political structures, and economic systems. He comes through disruptive prophets like Elizabeth Cady Stanton, Martin Luther King Jr., Desmond Tutu, Dorothy Day, and Pope Francis, who shake us up and call us to God's way of justice, reconciliation, and peace.

Three Gospels place this story just before Jesus' final journey to the cross. John places it at the beginning of Jesus' ministry to let us know from the start that Jesus still comes to shake human relationships, economic systems, and political structures in our world. He comes to purify us so that we can offer ourselves to God and to the world as an expression of God's goodness, justice, peace, and love.

In *The Lion, the Witch and the Wardrobe*, when the children first hear of Aslan they wonder if he is safe. Mr. Beaver replies,

"Who said anything about safe? 'Course he isn't safe. But he's good."[3]

PRAYER FOCUS

❖ What parts of my life need the purifying and refining fire of God's love?

❖ Where am I called to offer a God-centered protest to the abuse and exploitation in our world?

THURSDAY

DIVINE FOOLISHNESS
Read 1 Corinthians 1:18-25.

A country boy attended a formal dinner party. When the scalding-hot mashed potatoes touched his tongue, he spat them back out on his plate. Looking up at the other guests he said, "You know, some fools would have swallowed that."

That's evidently what folks in Corinth say when they hear Paul preaching about a crucified Christ. Paul uses the Greek word from which we get the word *moron*. The idea of a crucified savior is a contradiction in terms. You'd have to be a fool to believe it.

Paul says that some folks look for signs, miracles, or esoteric experiences. Others look for rhetorical wisdom that will confirm their assumptions or provide theological justification for their prejudices. But Paul dares to believe that the moronic word of the cross is God's power that is stronger than human strength and God's wisdom that is wiser than human knowledge.

Salvador Dali attempted to capture the mystery of Christ on the cross as fully human and fully divine in his best-known painting, *Christ of St. John of the Cross.* He said the sixteenth-century Spanish mystic Saint John of the Cross inspired him.

In Dali's vision, Jesus' body is perfect. No nails penetrate his hands and feet; there is no scar on his side. He hangs freely in front of the cross that soars above the world below. Everything moves toward and flows from his head at the center of the painting. This is the crucified Jesus who is at the same time the Son of God; the one of whom Paul said, "He is the image of the invisible God. . . . He himself is before all things, and in him all things hold together. . . . in him all the fullness of God was pleased to dwell" (Col. 1:15-19).

Ignatius of Antioch, who became a martyr in 115, opposed Gnostic wisdom that emphasized the divinity of Christ so strongly that it negated his humanity. He wrote, "Be deaf . . . to any talk that ignores Jesus Christ . . . who was really born, ate and drank; was really persecuted under Pontius Pilate; was really crucified and died . . . He was really raised from the dead."[4]

Cynics still say, "You'd have to be a fool to swallow that!"

PRAYER FOCUS

❖ When have you felt that there was something foolish about the cross?

❖ What does it mean for you to believe that Jesus on the cross is the Christ who is the center of the universe?

FRIDAY

FOOLS FOR CHRIST
Read 1 Corinthians 1:26-31.

An old Broadway song asks the question: "What kind of fool am I?" Immediately after acknowledging that the word of the cross seems moronic to the world, Paul turns his attention to his readers: "Consider your own call, brothers and sisters." Just as God chose to reveal divine wisdom and strength through the foolishness and weakness of the cross, God chooses to be at work in this world, not through the wisest, strongest, richest, or most impressive people but through ordinary people; people the world sees as foolish, weak, low, and despised. God works through those who are willing to become "fools for the sake of Christ" (1 Cor. 4:10).

When viewed through the lens of the world's wisdom and power, following Jesus looks downright foolish. It's no surprise to me that folks would prefer to post the Ten Commandments in the courthouse rather than the Beatitudes.

Blessed are the poor in spirit. . . .
Blessed are those who mourn. . . .
Blessed are the meek. . . .
Blessed are those who hunger and thirst for righteousness.
. . .
Blessed are the merciful. . . .
Blessed are the pure in heart. . . .
Blessed are the peacemakers. . . .
Blessed are those who are persecuted for righteousness' sake.
. . .
Blessed are you when people revile you and persecute you and utter all kinds of evil against you falsely. (Matt. 5:1-11)

On the basis of the world's ideas of wisdom and power, that looks downright foolish. These people are not the blessed in this world. These folks either get the short end of the stick or get nailed to one. The way of Jesus looks like weakness to those who think we can save ourselves and change our world by sheer human determination or through economic, political, or military power.

But for those who acknowledge their weakness as well as their powerlessness to save themselves, the cross becomes the sign of God's ultimate power. Those who know the limitation of their own wisdom discover the infinite resources of God's wisdom. People who willingly appear foolish in the world's eyes are often the people to teach others the way to be wise.

PRAYER FOCUS

❖ How does the idea of being a fool for Christ feel to you?

❖ What kind of fool are you?

SUGGESTIONS FOR SMALL-GROUP INTERACTION

❖ Play a video of "Was It a Morning Like This?" What emotions surface for participants as they watch and listen?

❖ How difficult do you find it to believe that the Resurrection is for the whole creation?

❖ Share a copy of Dali's *Christ of St. John of the Cross*. What do group participants observe?

❖ What part of the Lenten and Easter story do you find hardest to believe?

FOURTH WEEK IN LENT

∞

HEALING SCARS

There is more mercy in God than sin in us. . . . Just as love is stronger than death, so forgiveness is stronger than sin.

—William Sloane Coffin

SUNDAY

STIGMATA—THE SIGNS OF HIS SUFFERING
Read Luke 24:36-49.

The earth that shakes on Easter morning sits unmoving that evening. Still reeling from what they have seen and heard, the followers of Jesus hide in silence behind locked doors (John 20:19), shaking with fear and shivering with questions they cannot answer. With no angelical announcement, the risen Christ quietly comes among them. If this appearance resembles his appearance on the Emmaus Road, the disciples don't even notice his presence until he speaks, "Peace be with you."

The sound of Christ's voice scares the living daylights out of them. They have heard this voice speak peace to the rocking waves on the storm-tossed sea, but they assume it is a ghost or perhaps a trauma-induced figment of their muddled imaginations. To calm their fears and to confirm the reality of his presence, Jesus shows them the nail scars on his hands and feet.

It never ceases to amaze me that the risen Christ still bore the scars of his suffering. If God's power could raise Jesus from the dead, couldn't that same power have removed the repulsive reminders of the powers of evil, injustice, sin, and death that nailed him to the cross? But the scars are there; the unmistakable sign of his suffering and death; the eternal symbol of the ghastly cost of the world's salvation.

The Greek word translated "stigmata" describes a tattoo or brand used to identify a slave. Paul uses it when he writes, "I carry the marks of Jesus branded on my body" (Gal. 6:17). In medieval Catholic mysticism, the "stigmata" implied a spiritual experience in which saints received the scars of Jesus' crucifixion on their hands and feet.

The stigmata are a rare and questionable element in Roman Catholic tradition, but a medical dictionary defined stigmata as "cutaneous evidence of systemic illness." In our day the shrunken bodies of starving children, the maimed bodies of innocent people in war-torn nations in the Middle East, the lifeless bodies of Syrian refugees washing up on the coasts of Europe, and the blood-soaked bodies of the victims of our gun-addicted culture continue to bear horrifying evidence of the systemic illnesses of prejudice, xenophobia, greed, racism, and war.

Like the scars on the body of the risen Christ, they are the irrefutable evidence of the systemic evil that infects our human condition and the ubiquitous power of sin that contaminates our individual lives and the cultural, political, and religious systems of the world around us. No wonder Christians see the suffering of Jesus in the words of Isaiah:

> He was despised and rejected by others;
>> a man of suffering and acquainted with infirmity. . . .
> Surely he has borne our infirmities
>> and carried our diseases. . . .
> But he was wounded for our transgressions,
>> crushed for our iniquities;
> upon him was the punishment that made us whole,
>> and by his bruises we are healed. (Isa. 53:3-5)

Amazingly, those scars do not fade away after the Ascension. In fact, the stigmata on the body of the risen Lord stand as the eternal expression of the extravagant love and grace of God. Charles Wesley wrote these words:

> The dear tokens of his passion
> still his dazzling body bears;
> cause of endless exultation
> to his ransomed worshipers;

with what rapture, with what rapture,
with what rapture,
gaze we on those glorious scars!
—"Lo, He Comes with Clouds Descending" (UMH, no. 718)

PRAYER FOCUS

❖ What are the scars in your life? in our world?

❖ How can those scars bear witness to God's grace?

HYMN OF THE WEEK

"Crown Him with Many Crowns"

Crown him with many crowns,
the Lamb upon his throne.
Hark! how the heavenly anthem drowns
all music but its own.
Awake, my soul, and sing
of him who died for thee,
and hail him as thy matchless King
through all eternity.

Crown him the Lord of life,
who triumphed o'er the grave,
and rose victorious in the strife
for those he came to save.
His glories now we sing,
who died, and rose on high,
who died, eternal life to bring,
and lives that death may die.

Crown him the Lord of love;
behold his hands and side,
those wounds, yet visible above,
in beauty glorified.
All hail, Redeemer, hail!
For thou hast died for me;
thy praise and glory shall not fail
throughout eternity. (UMH, no. 327)

—Matthew Bridges and Godfrey Thring

MONDAY

SNAKES IN THE DESERT
Read Numbers 21:4-9.

Indiana Jones and I share a common trait. We both detest snakes. Having learned that about Indiana Jones in the opening scene of his first movie, we should have expected that before the end of the movie he would be trapped in an abandoned tomb where the floor was slithering with snakes.

Today's scripture reading recounts the bizarre story when poisonous snakes crawl everywhere at the Israelites' wilderness campsite. People suffer and die.

The backstory is that the journey to the Promised Land takes longer than expected. People look back with nostalgic amnesia on "the good old days" in Egypt, forgetting just how bad slavery was. They complain about bad water and lousy food—a dietary expression of their deeper rebellion against God and their determination to go their own way. The Bible calls it sin. As a result, they end up in a snake-infested desert.

When the people ask Moses to pray for God to do something about the snakes, God instructs Moses to make a bronze snake and lift it before the people. Those who have been bitten may look up at the bronze snake and be healed.

For the Hebrew storytellers, the snakes in the wilderness became a spiritual metaphor for the bitterness, resentment, and sin that poisoned their relationship with God. The bronze snake transforms the symbol of their sin into the sign of God's forgiveness. It's not unlike the way small doses of a substance that would otherwise result in death become the source of healing when the venom of poisonous snakes is milked to produce the antivenom that cures snakebite.

The bronze snake reminded them—and it reminds us—that the symbol of their rejection of God becomes the symbol of the extent to which God will go to save, redeem, and heal. When they look at the bronze snake, they see both the depth of their sin and the far greater depth of God's love and grace. The sign of death becomes the sign of new life.

PRAYER FOCUS

❖ What feelings does the Bible story generate in you?
❖ What "snakes" of sin slither about in your life?

TUESDAY

THE LOVE THAT LASTS FOREVER
Read Psalm 107:1-3, 17-22.

Remembering God's support of us in the past often allows us to experience God's love in the present. The reading from Psalm 107 looks back to the strange story of the serpents in the wilderness as a reminder that "[God's] steadfast love endures forever." In Psalm 136 that phrase becomes a rhythmic, congregational response, repeated in every verse. In this psalm, it appears as the call to worship as the congregation remembers how they have experienced that steadfast love in their history.

We see a familiar pattern in this recounting of the snake story. The people sin by rejecting God's way for their lives. They experience suffering directly related to their sin. In their desperation, they cry to God for deliverance. God hears their cry and responds in healing love, which breaks the cycle of sin and suffering. The people receive healing. In response, they celebrate in joyful confidence that "[God's] steadfast love endures forever."

Let's be clear that God's steadfast love was there for the people long before their experience with the serpents. God's love had already acted on their behalf, liberating them from slavery. God provided for their needs along the way. God's relentless love remains with them even when they reject it. Their rejection of God's design for their lives—not God's rejection of them—results in suffering and death. Their realization of their need and their cry for deliverance opens the way for the love that endures forever to become a present, healing reality in their experience.

A friend of mine suffered sexual abuse early in his life. That sinful act by someone else left a wounded place in my friend's life. But through the grace of God and years of healing therapy, he says that although the scar of the past still remains, it no longer defines or determines who he is and how he lives. With the people in the psalm, he gives joyful thanks for God's "wonderful works" in his life. He is living proof that the steadfast love of the Lord is forever!

PRAYER FOCUS

❖   When have you suffered as a result of sin?

❖   When have you discovered the steadfast love of God that lasts forever?

WEDNESDAY

THE BRONZE SNAKE AND THE BLOODY CROSS
Read John 3:14-21.

The strange story of the bronze snake is a peculiar text that might have remained in obscurity if the writer of the Fourth Gospel had not used it as an allegorical image of the cross. While most Christian people can recite John 3:16 from memory, most people skip over Jesus' words, "Just as Moses lifted up the serpent in the wilderness, so must the Son of Man be lifted up."

Just the way the snakes that caused death became the source of healing for the people in the wilderness, so the cross—the ultimate symbol of death—becomes the source of healing and hope for those who see in it the ultimate expression of God's extravagant love. The cross that reminds us of the depth of our sin becomes the expression of what Charles Wesley called "the depth of love divine, the unfathomable grace!" (UMH, no. 627)

Matthias Grünewald captured this paradoxical truth in the Crucifixion panel of the altarpiece that he painted for the chapel in the hospital where the monks of St. Anthony cared for victims of the plagues that swept across Europe in the sixteenth century. The most common disease involved poisoning of the blood system resulting in gangrene and open sores.

In Grünewald's painting, ugly lacerations, pustules, and sores cover Jesus' body. Some art historians say that Grünewald painted onto Jesus' body the same wounds that covered the bodies of the patients who worshiped in the chapel. When they looked up at the cross, they saw Jesus taking their pain, suffering, and death onto himself. When they looked up, the sign of their suffering became the sign of healing and hope.

As a pastor, I've had the painful privilege of being with people whose lives have been scarred by a broken or abused past. I've walked with them as they faced their pain. And I've seen them find hope when they recognize their own scars on the body of the crucified Christ and allow the love of God revealed in him to begin a healing process for them. Those same scars often become the healing gift they offer to others.

Just the way Moses lifted up the serpent in the wilderness so that people who looked up would be healed, Christ has been lifted up on the cross so that you and I, looking up to him, can be made whole.

PRAYER FOCUS

See from his head, his hands, his feet,
Sorrow and love flow mingled down.
Did e'er such love and sorrow meet,
Or thorns compose so rich a crown? (UMH, no.298)
—Isaac Watts

THURSDAY

RISEN WITH CHRIST
Read Ephesians 2:1-10.

After gazing at Grünewald's painting of the Crucifixion for three hours, Henri Nouwen said he experienced the cross as "the sign of the most radical transformation in our manner of thinking, feeling, and living. Jesus' death on the cross has changed everything."[1]

The second chapter of Ephesians explodes in praise for the way God's grace has changed everything. In the Greek manuscript, the first nine verses are a single, run-on sentence. The words overflow with exuberant gratitude to God who "out of the great love with which he loved us even when we were dead through our trespasses, made us alive together with Christ."

Throughout the passage, God is always the subject of the active verb. We are the passive recipients of God's grace. In the death and resurrection of Jesus, God has done something for us that we could never have done for ourselves. Just as God's power burst open the tomb on Easter morning, that same power has raised us to a new way of living that is energized by the Spirit of the risen Christ.

Beginning with the black smudge on our foreheads on Ash Wednesday, Lent is a season in which we remember that although we may be physically alive, we would still be spiritually dead in our sins were it not for the intrusive grace of God; God meets us wherever we are and loves us too much to leave us there. God's grace enlivens us to a radically new way of living and being. It does, in fact, change everything! John Masefield described his experience of that grace in his poem "The Everlasting Mercy."

> I did not think, I did not strive,
> the deep peace burnt me alive;
> the bolted door had broken in,
> I knew that I had done with sin.
> I knew that Christ had given me birth
> to brother all the souls on earth. . . .
>
> O glory of the lighted mind.
> How dead I'd been, how dumb, how blind.
> The station brook, to my new eyes,
> was babbling out of Paradise,
> the waters rushing from the rain
> were singing Christ has risen again.
> I thought all earthly creatures knelt
> from rapture of the joy I felt.

PRAYER FOCUS

❖ How have you experienced what Masefield described in his poem?

❖ How does the cross change the way you view your life and the world around you?

FRIDAY

BUT GOD!
Read Ephesians 2:1-11.

In Eugene O'Neill's autobiographical play, *Long Day's Journey into Night*, his mother looks back on her life and says, "None of us can help the things life has done to us. They're done before you realize it, and once they're done they make you do other things until at last everything comes between you and what you'd like to be, and you've lost your true self forever."[2]

We're easily tempted to think she got it right. We may assume that we can do nothing about what life has done to us. Folks who live miserable lives and make other people's lives miserable will often say, "That's just who I am. I can't change it."

The Ephesians probably believed that. Greek mythology assumed that fate controlled human life. You could do nothing about the gods' actions in your life.

By contrast, Ephesians declares, "But God!" God's immeasurable grace frees us from our old ways of living, which are determined by what the world has done *to* us. Now we live in a manner that reflects what God has done *for* us. By God's infinite mercy and boundless grace, our lives are being reoriented to the new life that is God's gift to us.

Though we may bear the scars of our past, we receive a new life that we did not create or manufacture by our own determination and effort. It is a pure gift of God that we accept with grateful joy.

During the struggle against apartheid, Desmond Tutu acknowledged that humanly speaking the situation often seemed hopeless. Then he went on to say, "But we are not alone. . . . The resurrection of Jesus is our guarantee that right has triumphed and will triumph over wrong, that good has triumphed and will triumph over evil; it is our guarantee that love has triumphed and will triumph over hate."[3]

Because of the Resurrection, our lives are no longer a long day's journey into night; they are an ongoing journey into light and life.

PRAYER FOCUS

❖ How have you experienced a "But God . . . " moment in your life?

❖ How far along this journey into life and joy are you?

SUGGESTIONS FOR SMALL-GROUP INTERACTION

❖ Read aloud Psalm 136 with one person reading the first part of the verse and the entire group responding with "for his steadfast love endures forever."

❖ Find a copy of Grünewald's painting of the Crucifixion and spend some time in silent meditation on it. Let participants share what they see and how the painting makes them feel.

❖ Invite those who wish to tell the story of the scars in their lives and bear witness to God's healing grace.

❖ Read aloud John Masefield's poetic witness to his experience of God's grace, and discuss how it speaks to the group.

∞

NEW LIFE IN THE GRAVEYARD

Easter is that moment when the laughter of the universe breaks through. It fades, of course, like a distant radio signal on a stormy night. A lot of noise and static crowds it out. But once we have heard it we know from then on that it is there. It is God's last laugh.

—Harvey Cox

SUNDAY

LAUGHTER AT THE TOMB
Read John 11:1-45.

What do you hear in the story of the raising of Lazarus? It would be hard to miss the desperate cries of the broken-hearted sisters, the funereal groans of the mourners, the weeping of Jesus at the tomb, and the tomb-shaking command: "Lazarus, come out!"

Eugene O'Neill heard something else. In his play, *Lazarus Laughed*, O'Neill imagined a dinner party in Lazarus's home after Jesus raised him from the dead. A dinner guest who witnessed the event reported the following:

> Jesus smiled sadly but with tenderness, as one who from a distance of years of sorrow remembers happiness. . . . Both [Jesus and Lazarus] smiled and Jesus blessed him. . . . and went away; and Lazarus, looking after Him, began to laugh softly like a man in love with God! Such a laugh I never heard! It made my ears drunk! It was like wine! And though I was half-dead with fright I found myself laughing, too!

When Lazarus describes his experience, O'Neill hears him say, "I heard the heart of Jesus laughing in my heart. . . . And my heart reborn to love of life cried 'Yes!' and I laughed in the laughter of God!"[1]

We've heard that laughter before. We heard it from Abraham and Sarah when the angel promised the improbable possibility of their having a child. And we heard God join the laughter at Isaac's birth. O'Neill imagined Lazarus hearing it as the voice that defeated death and brought him out of the tomb.

Death is, of course, no laughing matter. It's the truth we often attempt to deny, the truth we face with the imposition of ashes on Ash Wednesday, "Remember that you are dust, and to dust you shall return" (UMBOW, p. 323). It's the ruthless reality we face when we hear Jesus say, "It is finished" and feel the earth shake on Good Friday. It's the truth that Paul acknowledged when he wrote, "All die in Adam" (1 Cor. 15:22). The death rate among human beings continues to be 100 percent. The question is not whether we will die but how we will face it.

I hate death. I agree with Paul that death is "the last enemy," even when it comes peacefully at the end of a long and faithful life. But we face that inevitable enemy with audacious assurance that "death has been swallowed up in victory" (1 Cor. 15:26, 54). The Christian life is not a lifelong denial of death but a lifelong journey with the risen Christ in which we learn to face death's reality unafraid. Through life, in death, and into life beyond death, we know that we are not alone. We make the journey with a risen Lord who has made the journey before us.

I've never forgotten the story a seminary colleague who was the father of two young boys told. One day his sons went with him to the cemetery for a committal service. Before the family of the deceased arrived, the curious boys were peering down into the open grave. One asked, "Is that what happens when you die? They put you down into a hole?" Before my friend could come up with a biblically, theologically, age-level appropriate answer, the other son blurted out, "Yeah. That's what happens, but don't worry. Jesus is strong enough to get you out of that hole."

Both boys got it right. Paul follows his honest acknowledgment that we will all die with his resounding affirmation, "even so in Christ shall all be made alive" (1 Cor. 15:22, KJV). His affirmation fulfills the words Jesus spoke beside Lazarus's tomb, "I am the resurrection and the life. Those who believe in me, even though they die, will live, and everyone who lives and believes in me will never die" (John 11:25).

Father Robert "Griff" Griffin served for three decades as the chaplain at Notre Dame University. Anticipating his own death during a long, terminal illness, he boldly declared, "Death is a bully whose nose should be tweaked, and I hope to be one of the tweakers." With faith like Abraham, he never wavered in his assurance of the hope of resurrection. With laughter like Sarah, he wrote, "I want to be present at resurrections that defeat death's victories. . . . I want to greet death, when he comes irresistibly, with insolence and swagger, as though I were a baggy-pants clown to whom the final snickers belong."[2]

Followers of the risen Christ dare to believe that in the resurrection of Jesus Christ, God has tweaked the nose of the bully named Death, and we face death in the sure and certain hope that we will be among its tweakers on that resurrection day when the whole creation will laugh with the laughter of God.

PRAYER FOCUS

❖   How do you feel about death?

❖   How does the Resurrection connect with your feelings about death?

HYMN OF THE WEEK

"Sing with All the Saints in Glory"

Sing with all the saints in glory,
sing the resurrection song!
Death and sorrow, earth's dark story,
to the former days belong.
All around the clouds are breaking,
soon the storms of time shall cease;
in God's likeness we, awaking,
know the everlasting peace.

Life eternal! heaven rejoices:
Jesus lives, who once was dead.
Join we now the deathless voices;
child of God, lift up your head!
Patriarchs from the distant ages,
saints all longing for their heaven,
prophets, psalmists, seers, and sages,
all await the glory given.

Life eternal! O what wonders
crowd on faith; what joy unknown,
when, amidst earth's closing thunders,
saints shall stand before the throne!
O to enter that bright portal,
see that glowing firmament;
know, with thee, O God Immortal,
"Jesus Christ whom thou has sent!" (UMH, no. 702)

—William J. Irons

MONDAY

NOW AND THEN

Read 1 Corinthians 13:8-13; Jeremiah 31:31-34.

Greg was thirty-one years old when he died of non-Hodgkin's lymphoma. It came four months after being diagnosed, one week before his first wedding anniversary, and two months after the birth of his son. Preparing for the memorial service, I turned to Karl Barth, the most influential theologian of the twentieth century. He was also a father whose twenty-year-old son, Matthias, died in a skiing accident in the Swiss Alps. Barth's text came from today's reading.

> *Now* we see in a mirror, dimly, but *then* we will see face to face. *Now* I know only in part; *then* I will know fully, even as I have been fully known. And *now* faith, hope, and love abide, these three; and the greatest of these is love. (1 Cor. 13:12-13, italics added)

Barth said, "Because God's grace has come to help us in our misery through our Lord and Savior Jesus Christ. . . . We . . . stand with him at the border where the Now and the Then touch each other." Of Matthias, he said, "He has now crossed over it, and we are still here. But we are not far from each other if we put ourselves at this border. In Jesus Christ there is no distance between Now and Then, between here and there, however profoundly they are separated."[3] Barth pointed toward the fulfillment of the promise to Jeremiah, "I will be the God of all the families of Israel, and they shall be my people" (31:1), which Christ affirms in Revelation 21:3.

During the time of his illness, Greg's mother asked if he could hear her praying for him while he was in a coma. Greg replied that he could. He told her that he had simply prayed, "Jesus. Amen." Then he added, "Jesus is the King, you know." As Greg crossed the border from Now to Then, his brother told him, "Just go to Jesus."

We don't have answers for all our questions about death. Paul said it's like looking into a foggy mirror. That's where we find ourselves now. But the Resurrection holds the promise that then we will see clearly. On the boundary of Now and Then—faith, hope, and love sustain us. We know that God is with us.

PRAYER FOCUS

❖ In what ways does Barth's description of Now and Then speak to you?

❖ How can you take hold of the gifts of faith, hope, and love?

TUESDAY

LIVING IN THE WORD
Read Psalm 119:9-16.

The psalmist promised, "I will not forget your word." We invest time in learning scripture so that we will remember the words when we need them. It's the way the written word becomes "a lamp to [our] feet and a light to [our] path" (Ps. 119:105), even when that path leads "through the valley of the shadow of death" (Ps. 23:4, KJV).

The call came around 8:30 in the evening. Kay was a vibrant, active eighty-five-year-old, but her body could no longer survive the impact of the car accident a week earlier. Consistent with her end-of-life directive, there would be no heroic measures or last ditch, do-everything-you-can procedures. When I got to the hospital, I found her children and grandchildren gathered around her bed, holding her hand, waiting for her last breath. Now and then she would drift back into consciousness to acknowledge our presence.

A couple hours later, Kay turned to me and asked, "Jim, why does it take so long to die?" I replied, "It's a mystery to me. Maybe it's because we are so strong and have a hard time letting go." There were lighthearted moments when we remembered the woman in Proverbs 31:25 who "laughs at the time to come."

At 1:15 a.m., remembering our mutual appreciation of Shakespeare, she rephrased Hamlet to say, "To die or not to die, that is the question." I asked, "So, what's the answer?" She smiled and said, "Maybe not tonight."

It wasn't that night. Death came two days later. But it was what older traditions called "a good death"—death faced with faith; death that comes when we are surrounded by the people we love—but it is still death.

In a similar way, my mother-in-law died after a long battle with Alzheimer's disease. When she could barely remember the faces of her family, she could still quote, "I know whom I have believed, and am persuaded that he is able to keep that which I have committed unto him against that day" (2 Tim. 1:12, KJV). She never forgot the promise, and the One who made the promise never forgot her.

PRAYER FOCUS

❖ In what ways do you treasure God's word in your heart?

❖ What steps do you need to take to live more deeply into God's word?

WEDNESDAY

IN THE GARDEN WITH JESUS
Read Hebrews 5:5-10; Mark 14:32-41.

In times of personal meditation, I sometimes take an imaginary journey back to the Abbey of Gethsemani, the Trappist monastery in the hills of Western Kentucky where Thomas Merton lived. I imagine walking across the rolling pasture that leads from the Abbey to the woods where Merton built his hermitage.

The first time I walked that path, I was taken by surprise when I came upon a bronze statue of the three disciples, wrapped up in their robes, fast asleep beneath the trees. I felt like I needed to walk quietly so as not to wake them. A little farther along the path I found the bronze figure of Jesus in prayer. He is kneeling, but he is not bent over toward the ground. His back is erect; his face is lifted toward the sky. His elbows are in front of him and his hands cover his face. Gazing at the figure, I could hear the "loud cries and tears" as Jesus prayed "to the one who was able to save him from death."

The monastery placed the figures there in memory of Jonathan Myrick Daniels, a twenty-six-year-old Episcopal seminarian and civil rights worker who was assassinated in Hayneville, Alabama, in 1965. He died protecting a seventeen-year-old, black civil rights activist named Ruby Sales. I'm pretty sure that Jonathan would have prayed to be saved from death the way Jesus prayed in the garden. Neither Jesus nor Jonathan wanted to die. But I am confident that God heard their prayers and that both were made "perfect," meaning "complete" or "whole," through what they suffered. They showed us the way of self-giving love that leads to eternal life.

Just as Jesus wept at the grave of Lazarus, he again identifies fully with our human experience of loss, grief, and death in Gethsemane. He is Emmanuel, God-with-us, even in the darkest, loneliest, most God-forsaken hours of our lives. Jesus teaches us how to pray by offering to God the brutal reality of our broken hearts and struggling souls. He also shows us what it means to be "obedient to the point of death—even death on a cross" (Phil. 2:8).

Prayer Focus

❖   When have you prayed the way Jesus prayed in the garden?

❖   How have you experienced the self-giving love that Jonathan Myrick Daniels demonstrated?

Thursday

His Time Had Come
Read John 12:20-33.

When the Greek seekers ask to see Jesus, it confirms for him that his time has come. The "time" looms ahead of us the whole way through John's Gospel, beginning with the moment when Mary tells Jesus that the wedding party has run out of wine. He replies, "My time hasn't come yet" (John 2:4, CEB). But now, the time *has come* when he will become the finite, flesh-and-blood expression of the infinite love of God by going to the cross.

The time has come for Jesus to demonstrate the deepest paradox of the gospel. If we try to save our lives, protect our self-interest, hoard our gifts, and hold tightly to what we have, we will lose it all. But if we give our lives away in the love of God, release ourselves into something bigger than our self-interest, we will find life—life that is bigger than our own tightly confined existence, life that is filled with the infinite life of God. When we learn how to die, we learn how to live.

My father was fifty-nine years old when the doctors found three inoperable tumors in his brain and told him that his time had come. Without treatment, he might have six months to live. With treatment, he might have up to a year with a good portion of that time spent in the hospital.

He was a no-nonsense businessman. He weighed the cost-benefit ratio and decided that the payoff was not worth the investment. He taught us children that just because we can do something doesn't mean that we have to do everything.

As he left the hospital he told me, "I want you to know that I'm not going home to die. I'm going home to live as long as I can." And that's what he did. As his body weakened, he visited with old friends, tied up loose ends, and made arrangements for the end of his life. He even tried to bargain the cost of the casket with the funeral director friend who lived across the street.

I resent the fact that my father died so young. I know why Paul called death "the last enemy." But I give thanks that my father died the way he lived—not holding his life tightly but freely entrusting it to God.

PRAYER FOCUS

- ❖ What does it mean for you to lose your life to find it?
- ❖ How would you like to face death when your time comes?

FRIDAY

THE LAUGHTER OF THE UNIVERSE
Read Psalm 2.

The psalmist declares that God who "sits in the heavens laughs" at our human pretension and narcissistic arrogance. Dante heard that laughter in *The Divine Comedy*. As he ascended from hell toward purgatory, he hears a sound he described as *riso del universo*, "the laughter of the universe."

Suffering and death are not laughing matters. But if we believe the life-giving truth of Easter, we can hear—even in the dark shadows of death—the laughter that shook the earth on Easter morning, a laughter that will ultimately reverberate throughout the universe.

At one time people referred to the first Sunday after Easter as "Bright Sunday" or "Holy Humor Sunday." The tradition took root in early Christian theologians who said that God played a joke on the devil by raising Jesus from the dead. In the fifteenth century, churchgoers and pastors celebrated that Sunday as *Risus paschalis* ("Easter laugh") by playing practical jokes on one another, singing, and dancing. Pope Clement X banned *Risus paschalis* in the seventeenth century. The partying evidently went too far! But the divine laughter remains.

Because the infinite God is doing the laughing, this is not some polite little chuckle. It's cosmic laughter that shakes the heavens, leaves the angels in tears, and finds God nearly rolling off the throne. Because this is the God revealed in Jesus, we know the laughter is not mean, cruel, or cynical. It's laughter filled with love that comes from the same place as tears.

When I remember Dorothy, I remember her infectious laughter. When she was diagnosed with Alzheimer's disease, she and her husband faced her condition together with ruthless honesty, deep faith, and great love. Their witness became a gift to us all. Death finally silenced Dorothy's laughter even as it will finally silence ours. But by faith we dare to believe that the final joke is on death and that in the power of the Resurrection, Dorothy now shares in the laughter of God. And so will we!

PRAYER FOCUS

❖ How do you make room for laughter in your faith?

❖ How can you share that joy with others?

SUGGESTIONS FOR SMALL-GROUP INTERACTION

❖ Play the online video: "Abbey of Gethsemani—A Walk to the Statues" with your group. Ask the members to share their feelings about what they saw.

❖ Invite group members to tell which scripture reading or story in this week's readings touched them the most. Which one surprised them or made them feel uncomfortable?

❖ How does the idea of laughter in this context speak to them?

HOLY WEEK

∞

DESCENDING INTO GLORY

Hast thou not heard, that my Lord Jesus di'd?
    Then let me tell thee a strange storie.
    The God of power, as he did ride
    In his majestic robes of glorie,
    Reserv'd to light; and so one day
He did descend, undressing all the way.
             —George Herbert, "The Bag"

PALM SUNDAY

WHO NEEDS AN HUMBLE SAVIOR?
Read Mark 11:1-11.

Jesus must have looked downright foolish riding into the city on a donkey, his legs dangling down so that his toes scraped the dirt and his robe dragged in the dust. You can look important on a warhorse, but it's hard not to look like a fool on a donkey. The comic image raises some important questions:

- What if this story gives expression to the way God laughs at pretentious human pride? (Read Psalm 2:4.)
- What if the Palm Sunday parade is divine satire that punctures our pretensions of power?
- What if the man on a donkey is heavenly mockery of human might?
- What if the Savior is inviting each of us to get down from our high horses and follow him in the way of humility?
- What if an humble savior is not what we want but what we need?

The people who line the path that day shout "Hosanna." That Hebrew word means "help" or "save." It includes the imperative that gives desperate urgency to the cry. The crowd shouts, "Save us now!" They want a savior to come with military, economic, and political power to throw out the Romans and reestablish the throne of David. But that is not the kind of Savior God sent.

The peculiar story we tell this week demonstrates that God saves not through the exercise of loveless power but through the experience of what appears to be powerless love. God saves not through the myth of redemptive violence but through the model of redemptive suffering. God saves not by a rearranging of the world's political power players but by a radical reorientation of the human heart. God saves not by destroying those who oppose him but by forgiving those who nailed his Son to a cross. God saves not by escaping death but by going with us all the way to the grave.

The religious leaders laugh out loud at the joke: "He wanted to save others but he can't even save himself!" They don't realize that the joke is on them. Precisely because he refused to save himself, Jesus saved others.

We are fools to think that we can save ourselves. The joke is on us if we think that we can change the world by the sheer force of human wisdom and power. The man riding into town on a donkey and hanging on a cross may not be the savior we want, but he is the Savior we need.

The church I grew up in often sang the old gospel song "Love Lifted Me," written by James Rowe. It states the following:

Love lifted me!
Love lifted me!
When nothing else could help,
Love lifted me.

I never liked that song, but it happens to be true. The Savior I *want* is the one who helps me help myself; he is the one who allows me to hide my greed under a cloak of charity, dress up my political prejudices in a robe of religion, and parade through life on the stallion of pride. But the Savior I *need* is the one who comes in humility, who undermines my love of selfish power with the power of self-giving love, who calls me to get off my high horse and walk with him in the way of humility.

What if Palm Sunday actually is the day when the one who appears to be a fool turns out to be wiser than the rest of us? What if the man on the donkey turns out to be the one who puts everything else in proper perspective by looking like a fool? What if the foolishness of God is wiser than human wisdom after all? If we don't believe that, the joke may actually be on us. No fooling.

PRAYER FOCUS

Lord Jesus Christ, who comes tottering into Jerusalem on a donkey,

You are not the savior we expect.

Your power doesn't look like the power we want.

Your wisdom often seems foolish to us.

We are happy to join the crowd, waving branches,

but we're not ready to follow you

> into the temple court
> **into the upper room**
> into the garden of Gethsemane
> **all the way to the cross.**

Forgive our foolish assumptions.

Clarify our clouded vision.

Show us the foolishness of your salvation.

Hosanna! Hosanna! Save us, Lord. Amen.

HYMN OF THE WEEK

"O Love That Wilt Not Let Me Go"

O Love that wilt not let me go,
I rest my weary soul in thee;
I give thee back the life I owe,
that in thine ocean depths its flow
may richer, fuller be.

O light that followest all my way,
I yield my flickering torch to thee;
my heart restores its borrowed ray,
that in thy sunshine's blaze its day
may brighter, fairer be.

O Joy that seekest me through pain,
I cannot close my heart to thee;
I trace the rainbow through the rain,
And feel the promise is not vain,
That morn shall tearless be.

O Cross that liftest up my head,
I dare not ask to fly from thee;
I lay in dust life's glory dead,
and from the ground there blossoms red
life that shall endless be. (UMH, no. 480)

—George Matheson

MONDAY

THE WAY UP IS THE WAY DOWN
Read Philippians 2:1-11.

I'm not a surfer, but Scott is. He told me that if he faces a small wave, he can paddle over it. But if he sees a big wave coming, he has to go under it. When he does, he experiences a moment of calm beneath the wave. When he comes up on the other side, he can go on. But if he tries to paddle over it, he won't have the strength he needs to return to shore. His words remind me of the words of Isaiah:

> When you pass through the waters, I will be with you;
> > and through the rivers,
> > > they shall not overwhelm you. . . . ;
> Do not fear, for I am with you. (Isa. 43:2, 5)

Isaiah passed through the flood and fire with the assurance that no matter how deep the flood, the love of God is deeper still and God was with him.

In today's reading Paul lifts a hymn or affirmation of faith from the worship of the early church to describe the One who did not exploit his equality with God but came to be one of us. The words shake some of our common assumptions about the nature of God: "emptied himself . . . the form of a slave . . . born in human likeness . . . humbled himself . . . obedient to the point of death—even death on a cross." You can't go any lower than the grave.

But like an earthquake, the tectonic plates shift. God raises Jesus up and gives him "a name that is above every name." This one who descended is declared to be the Lord of all. The one who came down is the one who is lifted up.

In calling us to be of the same mind and have the same love as Jesus, the apostle challenges us to live in ways that move against the grain of our upwardly mobile, self-addicted culture. Paul calls us to nothing less than learning to live in ways that are consistent with the self-emptying love of Jesus Christ.

PRAYER FOCUS

❖ What difference does it make for you to believe that the One who was equal with God emptied himself of all but love?

❖ How have you seen or experienced the self-emptying love of God revealed in Jesus?

TUESDAY

WHY THIS WASTE?
Read John 12:1-11.

Everyone smells it. They all know it isn't cheap stuff. It is the kind of perfume a woman would use sparingly for special moments with the person she loved or might hoard as financial security for the future. But Mary squandered it! She poured it out on Jesus' feet.

Judas questions the sensibility of this action in John's Gospel. In Matthew's Gospel all the disciples ask the question: "Why this waste?" (26:8). The costly perfume would pay a year's wages for a common laborer. Why wasn't it sold and the money used for the poor?

It's the right question. It's the right question but the wrong time to ask it. Jesus' reply, "You always have the poor with you" doesn't minimize our responsibility to the poor. Rather, he defines the crucial ongoing practice of our lives. He sets Mary's extravagant gift in the context of God's extravagant love that will be revealed at the Cross.

Each Gospel includes some version of this story. John places it immediately after the raising of Mary's brother, Lazarus, and just before the entry into Jerusalem. In that setting, Mary's gift becomes her act of gratitude for what Jesus has done in her past and the precursor of what lies ahead. Her extravagant gift becomes the lens through which we see the extravagant love of God in the one who goes to the cross—her unspoken expression of immeasurable gratitude and love.

I remember a Good Friday service in our seminary chapel in which the academic dean preached. I'm sure he offered wise, scholarly words about the Cross, all of which I have forgotten. But I can't forget the way his voice cracked and his eyes filled with tears when, overwhelmed by the extravagance of God's love, he quoted Wesley's hymn:

> O Love divine, what hast thou done!
> The immortal God hath died for me!
> The Father's co-eternal Son
> bore all my sins upon the tree.
> Th'immortal God for me hath died:
> My Lord, my Love, is crucified! (UMH, no. 287)

PRAYER FOCUS

❖ How have you experienced the extravagant love of God?

❖ How could you respond in gratitude like Mary?

WEDNESDAY

A SERVANT IN THE HOUSE
Read John 13:1-20.

Daisy Bonner could have easily been forgotten if she had not scribbled some graffiti on the kitchen wall of a little, white-frame house in Warm Springs, Georgia. "The Little White House" was the place Franklin Delano Roosevelt (FDR) visited to escape the pressure of the presidency. It was also the place where he died.

Daisy was FDR's cook when he stayed in Georgia. She was preparing his meal when the brain hemorrhage struck that ended his life on April 12, 1945. It was his last supper. As an expression of her grief, she wrote on the wall: "Daisy Bonner cook the 1st and the last one in this cottage for the President Roosevelt." The words offer mute witness to her life of love and service to the president.

To most folks, Daisy Bonner was simply another black servant, like so many black women at the time, doing the mundane work of cooking and cleaning. But as I read her words, I heard the voice of a woman who had found her identity in what we could call "the ministry of the mundane." She did seemingly small things in a significant way because they made a difference in the life of one of the world's great leaders.

When Jesus gets up from the table, takes off his robe, wraps a towel around his waist, and kneels to wash the disciples' feet, he takes on the role of the lowest servant in the house—a servant whose name is quickly forgotten and who leaves no trace of his or her presence. When he says, "I have set you an example, that you also should do as I have done to you," he calls all his disciples to follow him in an unpretentious life of service that meets the needs of others. Washington Gladden heard that call and responded by praying:

> O Master, let me walk with thee
> in lowly paths of service free;
> tell me thy secret; help me bear
> the strain of toil, the fret of care. (UMH, no. 430)

PRAYER FOCUS

❖ Where have you seen the kind of servant life to which Jesus calls us?

❖ How are you following Jesus in the way of servanthood?

MAUNDY THURSDAY

A LAST SUPPER THAT STILL LIVES
Read 1 Corinthians 11:23-26.

Leonardo da Vinci's *Last Supper* is a beloved masterpiece, although little about it resembles Jesus' Passover dinner with the disciples. They would have been reclining on the floor. The table would have been loaded down with food and wine, including the roasted lamb that was slaughtered earlier that day.

But Leonardo never intended to paint a photographic image of a first-century Passover meal. He set the event in a typical fifteenth-century room so that people sharing dinner in the dining hall of the Convent of Santa Maria dale Grazie would experience Jesus' last supper as if it were happening in their own time and place.

When Paul repeats the story in our reading today, he does not expect the Corinthians to replicate the actual events of the upper room. He invites them to participate in the mystery of the way ordinary bread and wine become the body and blood of Christ. He calls us to believe that Christ joins us at the Table and enters our lives as we take the bread and drink the cup.

In a very different way, Salvador Dali expressed the mystery of Christ's presence in the Eucharist in his painting *The Sacrament of the Last Supper*. Like da Vinci, Dali brought the moment into the present by painting the view from his home on the coast of Spain in the background and giving it a mystical yet modern feel. White-robed figures around the table bow as the one at the center—the only one whose face we see—points upward to a transparent, almost ethereal torso floating above him with arms outstretched over the scene.

Because Dali's title speaks of the sacrament, I imagine the figures around the table as the saints who we believe gather with us when we share the sacrament. Perhaps the figure at the center is actually the priest pronouncing the liturgy over the bread and cup while pointing beyond himself to the invisible and yet very real presence of Christ whose arms are outstretched to welcome everyone to the feast.

However we imagine the Last Supper in the past, we affirm Christ's presence with us through the sacrament; the Last Supper still lives.

PRAYER FOCUS

❖ When have you experienced Christ's presence in Communion?

❖ How will you remember Christ today?

Good Friday

Earthquake at Noon
Read Matthew 27:45-54.

I acknowledge that there is nothing good about earthquakes. On August 24, 2016, a 6.2-magnitude earthquake struck central Italy. It reduced small villages to rubble. At least 247 people died and over 1,000 were displaced. Whenever and wherever they occur, earthquakes bring destruction and death.

Paul Tillich, a respected American theologian, published a book called *The New Being*. Here's the way he described the Good Friday earthquake.

> Nature, with trembling, participates in the decisive event of history. The sun veils its head; the temple makes the gesture of mourning; the foundations of the earth are moved; the tombs are opened. Nature is in an uproar because something is happening which concerns the universe.[1]

There was nothing good about the earthquake that shook the earth on Good Friday. The world turned dark because Golgotha marked the place where all the powers of evil, injustice, and death coalesced to nail the Son of God to a Roman cross. No wonder the earth trembled! But that same cross became the *cantus firmus* for all who follow Christ.

In music, the *cantus firmus* ("fixed song") refers to the consistent melody that works its way through the piece and around which the music moves. It provides the central theme of firm support so the music doesn't drift or go out of tune. It's the musical version of *terra firma*. A prime example is Bach's "Little" Fugue in G Minor.

I felt the *cantus firmus* when I listened to a voicemail that someone had left at 2:20 a.m. The person had been going through a difficult time; hopes had been shattered and heartbreak had struck home. Our journey together had contained moments of great joy, but now it led through a place as dark as noonday on Good Friday. Everything had been shaken. But the voice on the machine said, "I want you to know that the center still holds." My friend had found the *cantus firmus* of God's love in the cross.

PRAYER FOCUS

Behold the Savior of us all
nailed to the shameful tree;
how vast the love that him inclined,
to bleed and die for thee!

Hark how he groans! while nature shakes,
and earth's strong pillars bend!
The temple's veil in sunder breaks,
the solid marbles rend.

But soon he'll break death's envious chain
and in full glory shine.
O Lamb of God, was ever pain,
was ever love like thine? (UMH, no. 293)

SUGGESTIONS FOR SMALL-GROUP INTERACTION

❖ Listen for the *cantus firmus* in Bach's "Little" Fugue in G Minor.

❖ Ask participants to share personal memories of Holy Week.

❖ Discuss group members' observations on Dali's painting *The Sacrament of the Last Supper*.

❖ Include the video of "O Love That Wilt Not Let Me Go" as a part of your prayer time.

❖ Attend worship on Maundy Thursday and Good Friday as a group.

EASTER

∞

AFTER THE EARTHQUAKE

If Christ is King, everything, quite literally, every *thing* and every *one*, has to be re-imagined, re-configured, re-oriented to a way of life that consists in an obedient following of Jesus.

—EUGENE H. PETERSON

EASTER SUNDAY

NOTHING REMAINS THE SAME
Read Psalm 99:1-5; Mark 16:1-8.

One thing we know about earthquakes is that little remains the same after they occur. On December 26, 2004, a 9.1-magnitude earthquake shook the Indian Ocean, killing 230,000 and displacing more than 1 million people. The slippage of two continental plates along a fault line in the ocean floor caused the entire planet to vibrate. It was felt as far away as Alaska. Seismologists found that it actually changed the pull of gravity in that part of the world.

Matthew reported that early on Easter morning, "There was a great earthquake" (28:2). And nothing in this world has ever been the same! The Resurrection shifted the center of gravity in our lives so that everything we think about our world and our lives has changed. The empty tomb is God's confirmation that the way, truth, and life revealed in Jesus Christ is the way the whole creation will be saved. It affirms the words of the psalmist.

The LORD is king; let the peoples tremble!
>He sits enthroned upon the cherubim;
>let the earth quake!
The LORD is great in Zion;
>he is exalted over all the peoples.
Let them praise your great and awesome name.
>Holy is he!
Mighty King, lover of justice,
>you have established equity;
you have executed justice
>and righteousness in Jacob.
Extol the LORD our God;

worship at his footstool.

Holy is he!

Mark's Gospel doesn't describe the earthquake, but the women feel shaken when they see the effects of it: "The stone, which was very large, had already been rolled back." It's probably an understatement for Mark to describe them as "alarmed." If that wasn't enough to scare the living daylights out of them, they see an angel. When angels appear in scripture they always begin by telling people not to be afraid. Then the angel announces the earthshaking good news, "He has been raised; he is not here." He commissions these women to become the first witnesses to the Resurrection. And Mark notes, "They went out and fled from the tomb, for terror and amazement had seized them; and they said nothing to anyone, for they were afraid" (Mark 16:8).

It's a shabby way to end the Gospel. The other Gospel writers tell wonderful stories of the post-Resurrection appearances of Christ, but Mark closes with the disturbing picture of shell-shocked women running from the tomb in fear. It's even more awkward in Greek, where the sentence ends with a conjunction that should connect the previous action with what comes next. But nothing comes next. We're left with this dangling nonending of the story.

Some scholars think the last page of Mark's Gospel was torn off like the last page of an old book in a used bookstore. Then other folks tried to add better endings, turning the last pages of the Gospel into a patchwork quilt of different conclusions. But by most accounts, that's where Mark leaves us.

Mark's dangling sentence used to trouble me. But then I realized that in spite of my best efforts to pull the pieces together and bring a solid conclusion to every story, my life is full of incomplete sentences—relationships that get lost along the way, conflicts that are never reconciled, problems that never find a simple solution, stories with no last chapter.

Maybe Mark intends this ending. What if Mark is suggesting that there is something both amazing and frightening about knowing that the risen Christ is not where we expect to find him but is let loose in the world where nothing can stop him?

What if Mark's incomplete story serves as an invitation to every one of us to complete the Resurrection story with our own story? What if he purposely planned for every follower of the risen Christ to add his or her own chapter to the never-ending story of God's work of salvation in a sin-broken world? What if Mark intends for everyone who hears the Resurrection story to be sent—like those frightened women—to carry the good news to a world that never expected it? What if Mark's nonending is the call for us to get in on the action and become part of a story that never ends?

William Stafford (1914–93), American poet and pacifist, became the twentieth Consultant in Poetry to the Library of Congress in 1970. He developed a pattern of rising early every morning to write poetry while serving in work camps for conscientious objectors during World War II. Kim Stafford looked back on the life of his father in his book *Early Morning: Remembering My Father, William Stafford.* There Kim recorded these words of reflection: "My father quietly pursued the utter re-creation of the world. . . . My father saw his calling as both local and vast. My generation wanted to stop the particular war in Vietnam, while my father wanted to soften the hearts of the whole human family."

Kim cites a portion of William Stafford's poem titled "Believer." In it, Stafford affirms his intention to "live by the hum that shivers till the world can sing . . . when the right note shakes everything."[1] We who believe in resurrection are not called to sit around waiting to go to heaven or watching for a celestial return in the future. We are sent into the world to be the living, breathing, serving continuation of Christ's work until the whole world shakes with it.

Giacomo Puccini, one of the all-time great Italian composers, began work on *Turandot* in 1924 but died before he could complete it. Puccini's protégé, Franco Alfano, completed the opera based on Puccini's outlines.

The first performance was in Milan, on April 25, 1926. Arturo Toscanini, the greatest conductor of the time, held the baton. When they reached the point in the opera where Puccini's work ended, Toscanini abruptly stopped the performance, laid down his baton, turned to the stunned audience and said, "Here the Maestro died." He turned, walked away from the podium, the curtain came down, and the astonished audience went home with the uncompleted opera haunting their minds.

The next day the orchestra returned to the opera house and completed the opera with Alfano's ending. That's the way the opera's been performed ever since. A person who knows more about opera than I do told me there are other endings, written by other musicians, just the way other endings were tacked onto Mark's Gospel.

Mark's dangling nonending of the Gospel invites each of us to complete the Resurrection story with *our* story as we allow our lives to become a living witness to the presence of the risen Christ. It may be a shabby way to end a Gospel, but it's an earthshaking way to live!

Prayer Focus

Almighty and everlasting God, who in the Paschal mystery established the new covenant of reconciliation: Grant that all who have been reborn into the fellowship of Christ's body may show forth in their lives what they profess by their faith; through Jesus Christ our Lord, who lives and reigns with you and the Holy Spirit, one God, for ever and ever. Amen.

—THE BOOK OF COMMON PRAYER

SUGGESTIONS FOR SMALL-GROUP INTERACTION

❖ What is your most memorable Easter experience?

❖ What practical difference does the Resurrection make in your life?

❖ How will you participate in the ongoing ministry of Christ?

CLOSING HYMN

"Christ Is Alive"

Christ is alive! Let Christians sing.
His cross stands empty to the sky.
Let streets and homes with praises ring.
His love in death shall never die.

Christ is alive! No longer bound
to distant years in Palestine,
he comes to claim the here and now
and dwell in every place and time.

Not throned afar, remotely high,
untouched, unmoved by human pains,
but daily, in the midst of life,
our Savior in the Godhead reigns.

In every insult, rift, and war,
where color, scorn, or wealth divide,
he suffers still, yet loves the more,
and lives, though ever crucified.

Christ is alive, and comes to bring
good news to this and every age,
till earth and all creation ring
with joy, with justice, love, and praise. (UMH, no. 318)
                                              —Brian Wren

A Guide for
Daily Meditation and Prayer

[Prayer] is the practice of shifting preoccupation away
from yourself toward attentiveness and responsiveness to
God. It is a deliberate walking away from a me-centered
way of life to a Christ-centered way of life.

—Eugene H. Peterson

Developing your personal pattern of meditation and prayer
is like a jazz musician who, having learned the basic chords,
rhythms, and musical patterns, improvises to express his or her
own style, passion, and experience. Two essential elements in the
process are these: scripture and prayer.

Scripture: Feeding on the Word

In the Christian tradition, all spiritual discipline begins in
allowing the written word to become a living word in our lives.
Lectio divina, or divine reading, is an ancient way of reading
meditatively, always asking, "Lord, what is your word for me
today?" Here are the key elements of this approach:

* READ the scripture slowly. Watch for a key phrase or word
  that jumps out at you or holds special meaning for you.

- REFLECT on a word or phrase. Allow the word or phrase that you discovered in the first step to sink into your heart.
- RESPOND to what you have read. Form a prayer that expresses your response to the idea, then "pray it back to God." Many people find journaling to be helpful.
- REST in God's word. Let the text soak into your being, and savor this encounter with God and truth.

PRAYER: DANCING WITH THE TRINITY

Gregory of Nazianzus, the fourth-century theologian and archbishop of Constantinople, used the Greek word *perichoresis* meaning "rotation" or "dance" to describe the interaction of the three persons of the Trinity. In *A Disciple's Heart Daily Workbook*, my coauthor and I called the Trinity "a glorious dance in which the Father, Son and Holy Spirit are . . . in joy-filled, love-soaked, life-giving, never-ending movement together."[1] Learning to pray is like learning to dance. After learning the basic patterns of prayer, we grow into our own style. Experiencing prayer as a dance with the triune God invites us into three movements.

1. Praying with God the Creator (Father) begins as we center ourselves in the presence of God, who is so high above us that we can never fully comprehend God and at the same time so deep within us that we can never escape God. The psalms are particularly helpful in opening our lives to God's presence.

2. Praying with God the Son focuses our prayers in the likeness of Jesus, the incarnate God in human flesh. Our praying requires consistency with the words, will, and way of Jesus. We pray as Jesus prayed so that we may live as Jesus lived.

3. Praying with God the Spirit draws us out of ourselves and into God's ongoing work of love, justice, healing, and hope for our lives and for our world. We identify with the needs of others and listen for the ways we can become the agents of God's reconciliation.

Charles Wesley captured the dance of the triune God when he wrote these words:

Maker, in whom we live, in whom we are and move,
the glory, power, and praise receive for thy creating love. . . .
Incarnate Deity, let all the ransomed race render in thanks
their lives to thee for thy redeeming grace. . . .
Spirit of Holiness, let all thy saints adore thy sacred energy,
and bless thine heart-renewing power. (UMH, no. 88)

Welcome to the dance!

A GUIDE FOR
SMALL-GROUP GATHERINGS

Except for his appearance to Mary on Easter morning (Matthew 28:1-10), every appearance of the risen Christ occurs when the disciples are together: breaking bread in Emmaus (Luke 24:13-35), gathering in the upper room (John 20:19-23), sharing breakfast on the beach (John 21:1-14), and witnessing the Ascension (Matthew 28:16-20). The post-Resurrection stories indicate that although we may have unique individual experiences with Christ, it's more likely that we will know his presence in the presence of other disciples in worship, fellowship, and small-group sharing.

Small groups allow persons to share what they have discovered in the scripture readings, written reflections, and personal prayer during the week. The group leader does not lecture or teach but facilitates conversation. Here is a sample outline for small groups.

GATHERING

GETTING ACQUAINTED: In the first session, invite each person to share his or her name, one reason for participation in the group, and one memory of Easter. In following weeks, invite group members to share one new discovery they have made each week.

OPENING PRAYER/HYMN

OPENING PRAYER: The leader can offer the opening prayer each week, or it may rotate among the group members. It can be spontaneous or could be a traditional prayer from a prayer resource such as the the Book of Common Prayer.

HYMN OF THE WEEK: Share a recording or YouTube video of the hymn. Invite people to share what caught their attention or inspired them in the hymn. Keep in mind that the hymn noted for each week is a suggestion only. The group may prefer another selection; remain open to those hymns that speak to participants. Persons may actually be invited to bring meaningful music or art that speaks to them to the session.

FOR DISCUSSION AND REFLECTION

❖ What surprised or challenged you in this week's readings?

❖ Find a copy of any work of art mentioned in the week's study, and invite group members to share what they observe or how the painting makes them feel. As noted above, encourage participants to bring to the session other items that came to mind in association with the session.

❖ Use the additional suggestions included with each week's content.

❖ Speak aloud the next step each person will take to live into the week's learning.

PRAYER

- ❖ Share the way each member would like to be remembered in prayer.

- ❖ After a time of silence, go around the circle with each person offering a word of prayer or passing to the next person.

- ❖ Close by saying in unison the Mizpah blessing from Genesis 31:49: "The LORD watch between you and me, when we are absent one from the other."

NOTES

THERE WAS A GREAT EARTHQUAKE
Epigraph: Cornelius à Lapide, *The Great Commentary of Cornelius À Lapide* (London: John Hodges, 1887) 333.

THE INVITATION
1. N. T. Wright, *Surprised by Hope: Rethinking Heaven, the Resurrection, and the Mission of the Church* (New York: HarperOne, 2008), 23.

FIRST WEEK IN LENT: SHAKING THE POWERS
Epigraph: Paul Tillich, *The New Being* (New York: Charles Scribner's Sons, 1955), 178.
1. Maurice Sendak, *Where the Wild Things Are* (New York: Harper Collins, 1963).
2. John Wesley, *The Works of John Wesley*, vol. 27 (Nashville, TN: Abingdon Press, 2015), 28.

SECOND WEEK IN LENT: SURPRISING HOPE
Epigraph: Eugene H. Peterson, *Practice Resurrection: A Conversation on Growing Up in Christ* (Grand Rapids: Wm. B. Eerdmans Publishing Co., 2010) 8.
1. Frederick Buechner, *Telling the Truth: The Gospel as Tragedy, Comedy & Fairy Tale* (New York: Harper & Row, 1977), 49–50.

2. M. Scott Peck, *Gifts for the Journey: Treasures of the Christian Life* (San Francisco: HarperCollins, 1985), 126.

3. William Paul Young, *The Shack* (Los Angeles: Windblown Media, 2007), 95–96.

THIRD WEEK IN LENT: BEYOND BELIEF

Epigraph: Thomas Merton, *Life and Holiness* (New York: Herder and Herder, 1963), 162.

1. Wright, *Surprised by Hope*, 123.

2. C. S. Lewis, *The Lion, The Witch and the Wardrobe* (New York: Collier Books, 1950), 118.

3. Lewis, *The Lion, The Witch and the Wardrobe*, 75–76.

4. Ignatius of Antioch, taken from *Holy Women, Holy Men: Celebrating the Saints* (New York: Church Publishing, 2010), 642.

FOURTH WEEK IN LENT: HEALING SCARS

Epigraph: William Sloane Coffin, *Letters to a Young Doubter* (Louisville, KY: Westminster John Knox, 2005), 173.

1. Henri J. M. Nouwen, *Letters to Marc about Jesus* (San Francisco: Harper and Row, 1987), 28.

2. Eugene O'Neill, *Long Day's Journey into Night* (New Haven, CT: Yale University Press, 1955), 61.

3. Desmond Tutu, *The Rainbow People of God: The Making of a Peaceful Revolution* (New York: Doubleday, 1994), 39–40.

FIFTH WEEK IN LENT: NEW LIFE IN THE GRAVEYARD

Epigraph: Harvey Cox, originally appeared in *Christianity and Crisis*, April 6, 1987. Copyright by *Christianity and Crisis* (http://www.religion-online.org/showarticle.asp?title=485.

1. Eugene O'Neill, *Nine Plays by Eugene O'Neill* (New York: The Modern Library, 1921), 385, 387–88.

2. Luis R. Gamez, in *Great American Catholic Eulogies,* compiled by Carol DeChant (Chicago: ACTA Publications, 2011), 328.

3. Karl Barth, *This Incomplete One: Words Occasioned by the Death of a Young Person* (Grand Rapids: Wm. B. Eerdmans Publishing Co., 2006), 12–13.

HOLY WEEK: DESCENDING INTO GLORY

1. Tillich, *New Being*, 176.

EASTER: AFTER THE EARTHQUAKE

Epigraph: Eugene H. Peterson, *The Jesus Way: A Conversation on the Ways That Jesus Is the Way* (Grand Rapids: Wm. B. Eerdmans Publishing Co., 2007), 9.

1. Kim Stafford, *Early Morning: Remembering My Father, William Stafford* (Saint Paul, MN: Graywolf Press, 2002), 99.

A GUIDE FOR DAILY MEDITATION AND PRAYER

Epigraph: Peterson, *Practice Resurrection*, 162.

1. James A. Harnish and Justin LaRosa, *A Disciple's Heart Daily Workbook: Growing in Love and Grace* (Nashville, TN: Abingdon Press, 2015), 50.

ABOUT THE AUTHOR

THE REV. DR. JAMES A. HARNISH retired after forty-three years of pastoral ministry in rural, small-town, suburban, and urban congregations in the Florida Annual Conference of The United Methodist Church. He was the founding pastor of St. Luke's United Methodist Church in Orlando and served for twenty-two years as the senior pastor of Hyde Park United Methodist Church in Tampa.

Widely recognized as a preacher and writer, Jim is a facilitator for the Institute of Preaching at Duke Divinity School and the author of more than fifteen books including *You Only Have to Die: Leading Your Congregation to New Life*, *A Disciple's Path Daily Workbook: Deepening Your Relationship with Christ and the Church*, *Strength for the Broken Places*, and *Earn. Save. Give.: Wesley's Simple Rules for Money*. He served as consulting editor for *The New Interpreter's Dictionary of the Bible* and a contributor to *The Wesley Study Bible*.

Jim served on the board of directors for the General Board of Discipleship and the General Commission on General Conference, was a delegate to General and Jurisdictional Conferences and to the World Methodist Conferences in England, Brazil, Kenya, and South Africa. He is a member of the Board of Visitors at Duke Divinity School and the Board for Africa Upper Room Ministries.

Jim and his wife, Martha, have two married daughters and five grandchildren in Florida and South Carolina. He enjoys reading, travel, playing with his grandchildren, and cheering for the University of Florida Gator football team.

CPSIA information can be obtained
at www.ICGtesting.com
Printed in the USA
LVOW03s1048010218
564844LV00005B/5/P